*Way of Blessedness*

# Way of Blessedness

## Lord Stuart Blanch

**HODDER AND STOUGHTON**
LONDON SYDNEY AUCKLAND TORONTO

**British Library Cataloguing in Publication Data**

Blanch, Stuart Y.
   Way of blessedness.—(Hodder Christian
   paperbacks)
   1. Beatitudes
   I. Title
   226'.9306          BT382

ISBN 0 340 34643 4

Hodder and Stoughton Editorial Office: 47 Bedford Square, London
WC1B 3DP

# Contents

# Introduction

When the publishers asked me to write a book on The Beatitudes, they had in mind a companion volume to the book on the Ten Commandments published in 1981. It was a reasonable suggestion in so far as there is a clear connection between the law given to Moses on the mountain in Sinai and the new law given by Christ on a mountain in Galilee. But there the similarity ends. The Ten Commandments were, as other codes of law in the ancient world, negative in form and specific in application. The Beatitudes are not commandments at all, but a series of prescriptions for what is called 'blessedness' or as we might translate 'happiness'; they are statements of fact and they are allusive rather than specific in form. The Commandments were accompanied by the thunder and lightning of God's presence; the Beatitudes fell on the ear for the first time without any striking supernatural phenomena. The Commandments were given in the desert to Israel alone; the Beatitudes were offered to a mixed multitude of Jews and Greeks who were part of a cultivated and cosmopolitan society in Palestine. The dissimilarities are therefore more striking than the similarities. Moreover, the book on the Ten Commandments began as a series of broadcast talks for American radio where instant communication is the order of the day. This book permits of a more leisurely treatment and has to take into account a large and formidable body of scholarship which is unlikely to be familiar to the bulk of my readers. I have therefore tried to maintain a mean between academic discussion and practical application; practical application unless firmly grounded in academic scholarship is at the best meaningless, at the worst positively misleading.

The book therefore is divided into two parts. Part I concentrates on the background of the Beatitudes, seeking to expose the social, political, literary and spiritual environment in which they appeared and developed. Part II is a chapter-by-chapter exposition of the individual Beatitudes. You could be forgiven for omitting Part 1 and moving straight to Part II, either if you are already familiar with recent New Testament studies on the subject or if you are wholly unfamiliar, and indeed impatient, with them. But I think you will find that the study of the Beatitudes will raise academic issues on which you will need to come to a judgment or at least to form an opinion. By way of compromise, perhaps I could suggest that we follow the example of Dr. C.E.M. Joad who, in his popular-style books on philosophy in the 1930s, starred certain chapters 'to be attempted only at a second reading'. Part 1 would fall within this category.

I would like to express my gratitude to the publishers for their invitation to write this book which I certainly would never have attempted without their incitement; to Carolyn Armitage for her encouragement and for her assistance in making the manuscript ready for publication, to David Blunt, lay chaplain to the Archbishop of York, for reading the chapters in proof, to Lindsay Smith for typing the MS with exemplary skill and to my wife Brenda who has listened with unfailing patience to my preliminary reflections on the many academic and theological dilemmas I have encountered in the course of my own studies.

Passages quoted from the Apocrypha are for the most part in the King James' version. Elsewhere the version used is almost invariably the New International Version (Hodder & Stoughton 1979).

It has been a pleasure – and a pain – to write this book. There is bound to be pain in reading it too, but I hope pleasure as well. These sayings challenge our spiritual and moral pretensions at their root, and they open windows upon a view of life radically different from our normal perceptions of it. They are potentially revolutionary in their effect upon individuals and on communities. For the man or woman who takes these sayings seriously life can never be quite the same again.

* * *

*Part One*

# THE BACKGROUND

## Chapter 1

# JESUS THE TEACHER

It is difficult both for the author and for the reader to escape from the mental images conjured up by the name 'Jesus'. For some the name is invested with awe conjured up by centuries of tradition associated with stained glass windows, sacred music, ravishing art forms, and with impressive ecclesiastical occasions. Even the casual visitor to York Minster, for example, on an Easter morning, with the sun pouring through the windows, or on Christmas Eve with the first carol stealing on the ear, could hardly be wholly unaffected – and all this associated irrevocably with the name 'Jesus'. Even the busy tourist heading off to the next assignment will be aware of the bells ringing and catch a glimpse of that great building erected centuries ago to the glory of Jesus. Even the Christmas reveller who simply drives past on his way home and sees the crowds pouring into the Minster can hardly be unaware that something solemn and important is afoot.

The fact is that even in a society not obviously devoted to the Church and even in a society ideologically hostile to it, it remains true that 'Jesus cannot be hidden'; ancient folk memories arise, echoes of a long-forgotten childhood reverberate in the mind and we submit, however reluctantly, to its magic.

But for others the name 'Jesus' is invested not with awe but with contempt. This is the 'pale Galilean' who has destroyed man's delight in the natural life, a man over whose name ferocious religious wars have been fought, a man on whose behalf giant ecclesiastical structures have been raised, a man who cannot face up to the realities of the world. So Christians and non-Christians are in the same position – trapped in the mental images which they have inherited from the past.

It is all the more important, if we are to attend seriously to the Beatitudes, to achieve some objective view of the man to whom they are attributed in the pages of the New Testament. Otherwise those familiar words will, as it were, come to us down a long tunnel with little meaning or application – just impressive reverberations with no clear message for society or individual men and women. This chapter is therefore an attempt to make available to the reader who is either untutored in the Scriptures or over-familiar with them such information as we have or may deduce about the person upon whose life and words a whole superstructure of dogma and creed, of organisation and tradition has been built. Who is Jesus of Nazareth?

The first thing to say about Jesus, and especially so when we come to consider the meaning of the Beatitudes, is that He was a Jew, formed by His membership of a devout Jewish family, instructed in the Jewish synagogue school, and part of an ethnic and cultural grouping which we call Judaism. He was not an angel or a manifestation but a man. He was not quarried. He was born, so tradition avers, in Bethlehem and was brought up in the unprepossessing northern town of Nazareth. He was no heavenly being but a real person in a real world with brothers and sisters, uncles and aunts, with friends and enemies. He spoke, so we must suppose, with a northern accent. His hair was of a certain colour. He walked and sat and ate in a particular way. He did not lead a sheltered life in some religious community or other, but from His earliest days was associated with the trade and commerce and busy activity of a turbulent world. His father, so we believe, was a carpenter and presumably Jesus, as was the custom with Jewish boys, followed the trade Himself. We must discount the legends that grew up around Him in later non-canonical literature and make the point made in a striking way by the text of the Living Bible – 'He was only a local lad' (Mark 6: 3). And it is this factor, we are told, which almost wholly inhibited His subsequent ministry in His home town of Nazareth. Who could believe that there was anything special about this tradesman's son who swept up the shavings in the carpenter's shop and delivered the furniture and wrote out the bills? We have some knowledge of what an ordinary Jewish house was like in the first century:

> In many houses each couple had its own bedroom but in some cases all the members of the household slept in the same room. A kitchen was not a necessity in the house. When weather permitted all baking and cooking was done in the courtyard in the open air or under a structure. During the rainy winter season permanent ovens and stoves were also kept indoors. They were placed beside a wall below a window or with an outlet for the smoke to escape. Toilets were not found in houses, it was considered to be a luxury to have one even near one's house – they were normally only in courtyards and other public places. Among the common people an earthen floor was normal in both towns and villages. It was sprinkled with water and stamped down with an instrument or by foot.[1]

The home thus described would have been no different from countless other homes occupied by the peoples of the Near East and indeed such homes are still to be seen. But what was distinctive of the Jewish home was the spiritual and social regime under which life within it was conducted. From an early age Jesus would have been aware of the sacred festivals which dominated the Jewish year; He would have been reminded of that great day in the history of the world when Israel crossed the Red Sea dry-shod and began its long pilgrimage to the Promised Land. He would have been regaled with stories of Jewish

heroism and endurance in the towns and villages of the
Ancient World; He would know the names of those
described in the Epistle to the Hebrews who in the name of
their sacred religion 'were stoned, they were sawn asunder,
they were tempted, they were slain with the sword: they
went about in sheepskins, in goatskins; being destitute,
afflicted, evil entreated, of whom the world was not
worthy' (Hebrews 11: 37-38, R.V.). In the synagogue
school just down the road He would have been instructed
in the sacred Torah, the five Books of Moses, and would
have heard the Prophets read on the Sabbath Day. It is
likely that His first language was Aramaic but any Jew
wishing to make his way in trade or commerce would have
to be reasonably familiar with Greek, which was the
'franglais' of the Ancient World.

His home was the earliest influence on Jesus, as it has
been for most of us, but there was a wider world to which
He would have had access as He grew to manhood.
Nazareth was a town of Galilee, some seventy miles from
Jerusalem. Galilee was part of the Roman Empire,
Roman garrisons were everywhere and there may even
have been one in Nazareth. It was a populous country with
a comprehensive network of roads which facilitated a
brisk trade between east and west. Down the centuries
armies had marched and counter-marched over its hills.
From the time of Tiglath-Pileser III in 734 it had ceased to
be in any real sense Hebrew territory and until the end of
the second century was largely heathen with a relatively
small number of Jewish settlers within its borders. It had
been forcibly Judaised a hundred years before the birth of
Christ but was regarded by the orthodox of Jerusalem as a
place of little consequence. 'Galilee of the Nations' they
called it, mixed of race, uncertain of doctrine, and subject
to dangerous fanaticisms. Jesus' upbringing combined
the endearing piety of a Jewish home with painful
awareness of the dangers and excitements of the larger
world presented by the Roman soldier, the Syrian trader,

and the Greek Academy. The one who is now honoured by a thousand million Christians throughout the world and is worshipped in almost every nation began His life in 'Galilee of the Nations'. It was an upbringing at the same time calculated to inspire, to challenge and to chasten a young man who looked out upon the world from the doorway of His carpenter's shop. But there was nothing special about it.

Nothing special about it? But St. Luke records that:

> When he was twelve years old, they went up to the Feast, according to the custom. After the Feast was over, while his parents were returning home, the boy Jesus stayed behind in Jerusalem, but they were unaware of it. Thinking he was in their company, they travelled on for a day. Then they began looking for him among their relatives and friends. When they did not find him, they went back to Jerusalem to look for him. After three days they found him in the temple courts, sitting among the teachers, listening to them and asking them questions. Everyone who heard him was amazed at his understanding and his answers. When his parents saw him, they were astonished. His mother said to him, 'Son, why have you treated us like this? Your father and I have been anxiously searching for you.'
>
> 'Why were you searching for me?' he asked. 'Didn't you know I had to be in my Father's house?' But they did not understand what he was saying to them.
>
> Then he went down to Nazareth with them and was obedient to them. But his mother treasured all these things in her heart. And Jesus grew in wisdom and stature, and in favour with God and men. (Luke 2: 42-52)

The same author records that 'in the fifteenth year of the reign of Tiberius Caesar, Pontius Pilate being Governor of Judea, and Herod being Tetrarch of Galilee . . . the word of God came unto John the son of Zacharias in the wilderness' (Luke 3: 1-2, R.V.). Scholars are still divided upon the exact role of John the Baptist, as he came to be called, but there is a firm tradition that the emergence of

Jesus as a teacher was in some way associated with the ministry of John the Baptist and Jesus' baptism by him in the river Jordan. Jesus would have been aged then about thirty and we know nothing about the intervening years, between the visit to Jerusalem recorded by St. Luke and His public association with John the Baptist and the beginning of His teaching ministry immediately afterwards. Even at that early stage His teaching must have made a serious impression because when He returned to His own home at Nazareth and attended the synagogue on the Sabbath Day He was invited to read the lesson and took the opportunity of communicating to His fellow citizens of Nazareth the import of all that they had heard about Him:

'The Spirit of the Lord is on me,
because he has anointed me
to preach good news to the poor.
He has sent me to proclaim freedom for the prisoners
and recovery of sight for the blind,
to release the oppressed,
to proclaim the year of the Lord's favour.'
Then he rolled up the scroll, gave it back to the attendant and sat down. The eyes of everyone in the synagogue were fastened on him (Luke 4: 18–20).

The words in which Jesus described His own coming ministry were quoted from Isaiah 61 and their import was clear enough to excite violent opposition to Him in the town and to cause Him to leave Nazareth, so it is supposed, forever. Thereafter, so the synoptic writers suggest, He made His home in Capernaum, some twenty miles northeast of Nazareth on the shores of the Sea of Galilee.

It was only twenty miles from Nazareth, but the move represented a clean breach with the past. Jesus had learned the lesson that a prophet is not without honour except in his own home town amongst his own kindred. He had yet to learn the painful lesson later in His ministry that He could not trust even His own family, for it was they who wanted to take charge of Him, because they thought He was out of His mind.[2] But what was the source of the conviction which He expressed in the synagogue at Nazareth that He was 'anointed by God to preach good news to the poor'? There can be no authoritative answer to this question. We can only presume that the conviction emerged out of the inner life He lived with God throughout those so-called 'hidden years', that the decision to leave home and begin His own ministry was provoked by news of His cousin John's ministry in Judea, that He saw in the words of Isaiah a mandate for what He was now undertaking.

In one sense He was no different from the prophets of Israel whose calling was equally inward and equally mysterious. In other ways He was unlike the prophets of Israel in so far as He does not appear to respond to any particular political crisis or to be burdened with any particular concern for the state of the Jewish nation. He sets out to teach the 'Good News of God'.[3] So there was launched upon the world a teacher sent from God[4] who not only created an ineffaceable impression on the crowds who flocked to hear Him but predicted that heaven and earth would pass away but his words would not pass away (Mark 13: 31). We have yet to prove the truth of that utterance because heaven and earth have not yet passed away, but it is true that He remains one of the greatest teachers of mankind whose words men honour even where they do not understand or obey them.

New Testament scholars disagree about most New Testament issues, which is perhaps not surprising given the range of material which they are called upon to handle and the diversities of interpretation which date from the very earliest years of the Church's life. But I dare to say that on one issue New Testament scholars are almost wholly united – the primary relationship between Jesus and His followers was one of teacher and learners. For those rightly

sceptical of any unanimous opinon whatsoever the
following statistics are offered. The verb 'teach' is applied
to Our Lord's activity forty-five times in the Gospels. He is
described as a teacher forty-one times. He is addressed as
'Lord' (which was a title often give to teachers, equivalent
to the word 'sir' in some schools still today). The word for
disciple is a word more accurately translated as 'learner'
and that is used 200 times. People were puzzled by His
origin and His identity; some took Him to be a prophet, at
least one potentate in Israel thought Him to be John the
Baptist risen from the dead, and others thought Him the
promised Elijah returned to herald the Day of the Lord.
But Nicodemus, himself a teacher in Israel, was expressing
more than his own opinion and reflecting the opinions of
many in his own class when he said that Jesus was a
teacher sent from God. But we must be more specific and
ask the question – a teacher of what?

Here you must permit me to make a slight deviation to
take account of what Anthony Harvey in the Bampton
Lectures of 1980 called 'the constraints of history'.[5] Amidst
all the constraints – political, cultural, theological –
within which Jesus as a man of His time had to live was
the assumption that dominated Judaism, viz. that the
whole of Jewish life was based on the validity and
importance of the Law. It is extremely unlikely that Jesus
contemplated an attack on this basic institution; indeed
He was remembered as having been present in the
synagogue Himself on numerous occasions.[6] It follows
that no teacher would have been capable of commanding a
hearing either amongst the ordinary people or amongst
the intelligentsia of Israel if he had not taken this
convention seriously. This is borne out by study of the
language used both in the Old Testament and in the New.

I was once bold enough in an address to a Jewish
audience which contained many Rabbis to say that the
Hebrew word normally translated 'teach' is almost
invariably used, where no object is provided to the verb, to

signify the teaching of the Law. I was relieved to be told by one of the younger Rabbis afterwards that this observation was wholly correct. Jesus then was regarded as, and could not but have regarded Himself as, a teacher of the Law. His method of teaching as we shall see was different from but not entirely alien to the methods employed by the Rabbis of His era.[7] I cannot prove it because my own studies are incomplete, but I have an inkling that the parables for which Jesus is justly famous have a bearing in almost every case upon some aspect of the already existent Law of Moses. So Jesus was a Rabbi amongst other Rabbis. He is addressed as Rabbi on fifteen occasions and as Rabboni (a particularly honorific form of address) twice. St. Matthew suggests that He wore the kraspedon ('the hem of his garment') which was as distinctive of a Rabbi as a dog-collar would be distinctive of a clergyman today. In a manner familiar to His contemporaries He gathered to Himself twelve disciples representing the Twelve Tribes of Israel, living together under a common rule with a common purse. Jesus of Nazareth was no way-out evangelist, no eccentric guru, but one who was regarded by the public and indeed by some members of the Rabbinic establishment as a teacher of the Law sent from God. In a sense this was 'no constraint', the Law was the only vehicle He had, the Law was the only source to which He could appeal; Law, so He believed, was from God and not one jot or one tittle of it could be ignored.

It was necessary to establish this point before going on to say that the evidence of the Gospels is that He was a wholly exceptional teacher of the Law; whose style of life and utterance was different from other Rabbis; who had a paradoxical way of speaking which imprinted itself so deeply on the traditions concerning Him that many of His words and illustrations are still available to us two thousands years after they were first uttered. T:W. Manson, to whose writings I owe a great personal debt, whilst acknowledging the similarities of Our Lord's method with those current in His time, isolated what he called two important features which made His teaching distinctive – the use of poetic form and His teaching in parables. I quote from his book *The Sayings of Jesus* (p.31):

> A characteristic feature of this kind of poetry is what is known as parellelism or the rhyming of thoughts. In an English heroic couplet we look for a correspondence in two lines, first in the number of stressed syllables and then in the sound of the final syllables. In a pair of Latin hexameters we expect a certain amount of correspondence in the arrangement of long and short words. In the Hebrew couplet there is a certain correspondence of rhythm and, most important, a correspondence in thought.[8]

The same point is made by an equally distinguished scholar, Dr. Matthew Black, in his book *An Aramaic Approach to the Gospels and Acts*.[9] It is interesting that he should take the Beatitudes as one of his examples of Hebrew poetry. But there are many other examples of the poetic form of Our Lord's teaching in all four Gospels.

The other feature of Our Lord's teaching, the parabolic form, was once thought to be highly distinctive of Him but scholars are less certain now, and are prepared to allow that the parabolic form was not entirely unknown in the teaching of the Rabbinic schools. But perhaps there are three other features in addition to the ones noted by Dr. Manson that at least appear to be distinctive of Jesus' teaching and I mention them briefly without pressing you with the evidence.

First, the normal method of teaching employed by the Rabbinic schools rested heavily on an appeal to precedent. In order to substantiate the point to win an argument an appeal had to be made to one of the teachers of the past, to a name already honoured in Israel as one of the great. [10] Although Our Lord was clearly aware of other points of view, especially in His sayings about divorce, He does not appeal to them as authoritative. His authority is from above. Second, although He is a teacher of the Law and counsels obedience to it He exercises a certain royal freedom in the exposition of it which on occasion goes far back beyond even Moses to the original revelation to Abraham and even to the creation of the world. In this sense He could be described as a radical teacher of the Law, radical used in its proper sense, as going back to the roots of the tradition in the earliest pages of Scripture. Thirdly, His verbal arguments are often clinched by a healing-saving action, as in the so-called conflict stories,[11] or in the healing of the blind man in St. John's Gospel. In this, of course, He is reminiscent of Moses himself who not only taught the law in the wilderness but guided Israel through the wilderness with many signs and portents.

Jesus like every other teacher was subject to 'the constraints of history'. Some of His movements about the countryside were dictated by political considerations. He was on occasion challenged to make political judgments. Interlocutors sought to trap Him in the religious controversies of His day. But above all He was the child of a particular culture and He would not have been heard if He had not spoken out of that culture to the people who shared that culture. Every allowance has to be made for the fact that He was not always speaking to people who adhered to the faith of His fathers. The crowds included adherents of the mystery religions of His day, foreigners and aliens, Romans and heathens, Palestinians and Greeks, fanatical Jews, and Jews who had lost all contact with their ancestral religion. If a teacher does not speak the language of the people the people will not hear him, charm he ever so wisely. The remarkable feature of Our Lord's teaching was not only that the people of His day heard Him gladly[12] but that people every bit as heterogeneous in culture and education have been hearing Him gladly ever since. This calls for some explanation. The Christian's explanation is that Jesus was a teacher 'sent from God'. He will want to say much more but he can hardly say less. The non-Christian or the half-persuaded Christian who happens upon this book will have to judge for himself whether that claim is justified. If it is justified such a reader will have to consider further the implications of that belief for himself and for the ordering of the society to which he belongs.

## Chapter 2

# MATTHEW THE INTERPRETER

When the bomb went off outside Harrods just before Christmas 1983 it did not take long to establish what you might call the 'facts'. That same evening on the television news we knew what time the bomb exploded, we knew the size of the bomb and the registered number of the car in which it was placed. Sadly, we also knew the number of the dead and injured and the condition of those still in hospital. But a visitor from the New Hebrides or from Taiwan would have known nothing, even when told of the so-called facts. Behind those bare facts, as we know only too well, lies a long history of repression and violence, misunderstanding and recrimination, without which the event is inexplicable. But history can only be written by historians, and historians cannot be other than they are, men of like passions as ourselves – prejudiced, enthusiastic for a cause, conditioned by cultural background and personal disposition. Thus, no two historians will agree about what really 'happened' outside Harrods just before Christmas 1983.

The main events connected with the life of Jesus of Nazareth can be briefly and convincingly related. He was brought up in Nazareth and educated in a local synagogue school. At the age of thirty or thereabouts, He left his parental home and established some sort of base in nearby Capernaum. From there He conducted a series of teaching and healing missions in the countryside of Galilee. He was

enthusiastically received by the people of the land, but
even at that stage encountered a certain amount of
opposition from representatives of official Judaism sent
down from Jerusalem. He gathered to Himself a
substantial group of interested men and women, and from
that group selected twelve men to be His companions for
the rest of His life on earth. Opinions vary as to how many
times He went up to Jerusalem, but it is certain that He
went up to Jerusalem some three years after He began His
public ministry. There He was engaged in public
controversy with the leaders of His people, was arrested
and had His case referred to Pontius Pilate, the Roman
Governor. He was examined under the lash, and was
crucified.

There is no serious dispute about these facts. But there is
another fact which is endlessly disputed because it will not
conform to the ordinary categories of historical writing.
He was crucified on Friday afternoon, and was buried in a
local sepulchre. On the following Sunday morning the
tomb was empty, and subsequently His twelve chosen
companions asserted that He was risen from the dead and
had appeared to a great number of His disciples under
varying circumstances – on the road to a village called
Emmaus, in a house already familiar to the disciples in
Jerusalem, and on the shores of Lake Galilee. Of these
appearances there are up to eleven distinct accounts in the
New Testament. It is easy to see why this culminating
event of His life should have been the subject of such fierce
argument. It was an event without precedent and without
parallel. The secular historians' view therefore is that it
could not have happened at all, and we must substitute for
it some general hallucination or some private vision. But
there is another fact which is beyond dispute. The Church
exists, divided and inadequate no doubt, but still the
greatest organisation here on earth, present in every ethnic
and language group, influential still in political and
social life, and visible on the ground in the majestic

architectural structures in which it worships. This is a far cry indeed from those squalid manoeuvres by which Jesus of Nazareth was tracked down, and ultimately done to death. It is a far cry from the little group of frightened men, huddled together in a Jerusalem house for fear of the Jews. The secret of the Church's continuous existence is proclaimed on Easter Sunday year after year – 'Christ is risen; He is risen indeed.' No casual visitor to a parish church or a cathedral can hear a huge congregation join in that response without at least permitting himself the thought that it could after all be true.

I permit myself this excursus on the life and death and resurrection of Jesus of Nazareth, because the reader needs to know that it was in the light of this resurrection truth that all the events leading up to it were subsequently to be interpreted. So it could be said of the Gospel writers – and they would be honoured by this assertion – they were not objective historians; they were heavily biased by the events through which their predecessors in the faith had lived. They took it for granted that Jesus of Nazareth was risen from the dead and that, to use a familiar oriental imagery, He was seated at the right hand of God and would return at the end of time to judge the world. In their view a little man from the little-regarded town of Nazareth was King of all Kings, Lord of all Lords. This was a staggering belief and was to animate the lives of millions upon millions of those who shared that belief.

The author of the first Gospel, as indeed the authors of the other three Gospels, was an interpreter; the Gospel is 'according to St. Matthew'. There is no claim in the text itself that Matthew, the tax gatherer and apostle, was the author of the Gospel. That claim rests on second-century tradition represented by Papias, a bishop of Hierapolis, in Asia Minor. In a statement attributed to him by the historian Eusebius, he said that 'Matthew the Apostle compiled certain oracles in the Hebrew language, and everyone translated them according to his ability.' There is nothing intrinsically unlikely about that statement, but it by no means constitutes a claim for the apostolic authorship of the whole Gospel. There is no reason, either, why these oracles could not have been incorporated in the Gospel which we have before us, and this would account for the fact that the Gospel came to be known as the 'Gospel according to St. Matthew'.[1] Valiant attempts are still made, for example, by Doctor Butler,[2] to establish the chronological priority of St. Matthew, but the great bulk of opinion still adheres to the view that the author of St. Matthew's Gospel adopted an outline of Jesus' life already available to him in St. Mark's Gospel. It is a fact that ninety per cent of St. Mark's Gospel is incorporated in St. Matthew, sometimes with only minor verbal alterations. This fact alone must challenge the claim that St. Matthew's Gospel was the first. If it had been composed by Matthew the Apostle, he would have had an intimate knowledge of Jesus' life and ministry, and would not have had to depend so slavishly on an outline by someone who possessed no such knowledge.

If therefore we are to attempt any understanding of the Sermon on the Mount in general, and the Beatitudes in particular, we now have to ask certain questions about the anonymous author who sat down in the latter part of the first century with a copy of St. Mark's Gospel in front of him, and proceeded to write his own. Why did he write a Gospel of his own anyway? What were his sources? What models did he have in mind? What can we discover about his environment? What may we deduce about his main theological and practical interests? Even when we have done all this and then turn to the Sermon on the Mount and the Beatitudes, we shall still be looking through a glass darkly, but we shall have faced the questions.

The first question, then, why did he write a Gospel at all? Writing in the ancient world was a laborious process – without benefit of typewriters, word processors, dictating machines and proof readers. There was no money in it, no royalties, no public lending rights, no literary lunches, no publishers, no reviewers. The author who put pen to paper in the Ancient World would have done so only out of a burning desire to communicate a message or to achieve modest fame. But no fame was attached to the writing of what we call a 'Gospel', which in its exact form is without parallel or precedent in the Ancient World, which commanded no ready market, and was unlikely to circulate in the academic establishments of Asia Minor or Greece. The author of the first Gospel, therefore, could only have been writing because he had something to say to the local church (wherever that was) to which he belonged. He would not have been writing at all if everything he had to say had been said before. It follows that he must for some reason have been dissatisfied with the Gospel according to St. Mark. It is easy to see why Matthew (I use the name for the sake of simplicity) felt that St. Mark's Gospel needed supplementing. The most serious lack in that Gospel was that it contained no accounts of the resurrection appearances. This is not apparent if you are using the Authorised Version of the Bible. You will need to know that the earliest and most reliable text of this Gospel ended at Chapter 16: 8; the ending quoted in the Authorised Version has been supplied from some other document no longer available to us. I need not weary you with the suggestions that have been made to account for the strange fact that the first Gospel ended with the words 'neither said they anything to any man, for they were afraid.' Was the manuscript damaged? Was it just at that point that Mark heard a knock on the door in the night to find Roman soldiers on the doorstep? Did he die suddenly? or did he actually intend his bequest to the world to end there? These questions are unanswerable now, and they were probably unanswerable in Matthew's time; he just felt that an ending of that kind did not do justice to the convictions of the Church or to the status of the earlier apostles, whose authority rested on the fact that they had seen Jesus of Nazareth alive after His burial.

When Matthew wrote, we may presume that every local or regional church had some deposits of tradition well established in its liturgy and teaching. Matthew therefore recorded the resurrection appearances current in his church, St. Luke in his and St. John in his. They are not incompatible with each other, but neither can they be easily harmonised. However, in Matthew's view they were essential – to the faithful proclamation of the Gospel and to the convictions already represented in the Church relating to the life, death and resurrection of Jesus. But the traditions current in Matthew's church also included certain views about the origins and early life of Jesus, of which St. Mark's Gospel took no cognisance whatsoever. If the Church had had to rely on Mark's Gospel, there would have been no stable in Bethlehem, no shepherds in the fields, no angelic message, no wise men; there would have been no 'Christmas' as we understand it now. Mark had no time or space for these things, and was content to begin his Gospel with those triumphant words 'The beginning of the Gospel of Jesus Christ the Son of God.' So Matthew supplied an end and a beginning. But he would have observed, too, that Mark's Gospel was strangely deficient in records of Jesus' teaching. Mark has only nine parables, Matthew has twenty-one, Luke has twenty-seven. It is difficult to imagine how the preaching and teaching of the Church could have developed as it has without these valuable additions to the Marcan narrative. Without Matthew there would have been no Sermon on the Mount and no Beatitudes.

Now we turn to the second question: where did Matthew derive all his additional material? – a question which has exercised the minds of generations of scholars and students. You will not be surprised to know that there is no wholly agreed answer to this question. The most familiar explanation is that Matthew had in front of him not only a version of St. Mark's Gospel, but a document entitled 'Q' which included sayings and parables, and may have

incorporated what Papias described as 'the Oracles' of the
Apostle Matthew. This document 'Q' has, it needs to be
said, no concrete existence. It is a deduction from the
careful study of the non-Marcan material in Matthew and
Luke and a conviction that both Matthew and Luke had
access to the same common document. There is nothing
intrinsically unlikely about this theory, but it is, and will
forever be incapable of proof. In addition, Matthew would
have in front of him material which is now peculiar to his
Gospel and it must be presumed was known to him from
the traditions of the Church to which he belonged.

This theory of the source of Matthew has been heavily
attacked and many alternatives to it have been suggested.
But for our immediate purpose, the important thing is
that Matthew's decision to write was based upon
dissatisfaction with the only other Gospel he had, and
upon his possession of certain traditions which might
otherwise never have survived. But this begs one very
important question. It could be that Mark's Gospel was
'deficient' by intent. Mark belonged to a Church which
lived not just on the basis of a past event, but on the basis of
a future consummation: the return of The Lord in Glory.
The last words of Mark 13 are significant for the attitude of
the community to which he belonged:

> No-one knows about that day or hour, not even the angels in
> heaven, nor the Son, but only the Father. Be on guard! Be alert!
> You do not know when that time will come. It's like a man
> going away. He leaves his house and puts his servants in
> charge, each with his assigned task, and tells the one at the
> door to keep watch.
>     Therefore keep watch because you do not know when the
> owner of the house will come back – whether in the evening, or
> at midnight, or when the cock crows, or at dawn. If he comes
> suddenly, do not let him find you sleeping. What I say to you, I
> say to everyone. 'Watch!' (Mark 13: 32–37)

These words were written before the fall of Jerusalem in
A.D.70. It was a common opinion in the early Church,

based on the received utterances of Jesus Himself, that the fall of the ancient city of Jerusalem would herald the return of the Messiah. But when Matthew was writing Jerusalem had fallen; every stick and stone had been overturned, the Jewish community had been dispersed and the Christians with them. The 'joy of the whole earth' was now the habitation of owls and foxes and birds of prey. There had been no sign from Heaven and the Messiah had not returned. This was bound to cause a sea-change in the life and thought of the early Christian communities, and one change was that leaders of the Church began to think in terms of a longer period between the first coming of Christ and the second; they had to allow for the possibility that the Church had a longer work to do on earth than they had expected – and this at the same time as they had to maintain an attitude of expectancy laid upon them by the words of Jesus Himself – 'What I say unto you, I say unto all, watch.'

If it is agreed that St. Matthew was writing after the fall of Jerusalem, the 'survival' of certain valuable traditions would have seemed to him more important than they could ever have seemed to St. Mark who was writing before the fall of Jerusalem. Matthew had in view a longer process of preaching and teaching and evangelism. That is evident from the way in which he ends the Gospel:

> Therefore go and make disciples of all nations, baptising them in the name of the Father and of the Son and of the Holy Spirit, and teaching them to obey everything I have commanded you. And surely I am with you always, to the very end of the age. (Matthew 28: 19-20)

If the author was, as is sometimes suggested, a bishop in Syria, we must congratulate him on having preserved in his own mind a fervent expectation of the return of the Messiah (Matthew 24) together with a proper episcopal concern for the longer future of the Church.

Now we turn to the third question listed above and ask what models Matthew had in mind when he attempted this unprecedented task of writing a new Gospel. Even the most casual reader will have observed Matthew's intense preoccupation with the Old Testament. John has fourteen quotations from the Old Testament, Luke has twenty-two, Mark has twenty-five and Matthew has forty-seven. These figures speak for themselves, and are even more impressive when it is realised that apart from actual quotations Matthew has innumerable references to Old Testament symbol and imagery. The Book of Deuteronomy, for example, has an elevated and lofty style recounting the last discourse of Moses, which Matthew may have wished to emulate. He may have seen himself engaging in an exercise not dissimilar to that of the Chronicler as that unknown writer reshaped and enriched the work of his predecessor, the author of 1 and 2 Kings. Or he may have seen himself as the pious scribe of the Apocryphal book, Ecclesiasticus:

> But he that giveth his mind to the law of the most High, and is occupied in the meditation thereof, will seek out the wisdom of all the ancient, and be occupied in prophecies.
> He will keep the sayings of the renowned men: and where subtil parables are, he will be there also.
> He will seek out the secrets of grave sentences, and be conversant in dark parables.
> He shall serve among great men, and appear before princes: he will travel through strange countries; for he hath tried the good and the evil among men.
> He will give his heart to resort early to the Lord that made him, and will pray before the most High, and will open his mouth in prayer, and make supplication for his sins.
> When the great Lord will, he shall be filled with the spirit of understanding: he shall pour out wise sentences, and give thanks unto the Lord in his prayer.
> He shall direct his counsel and knowledge, and in his secrets shall he meditate.

He shall shew forth that which he hath learned, and shall glory in the law of the covenant of the Lord.

Many shall commend his understanding; and so long as the world endureth, it shall not be blotted out; his memorial shall not depart away, and his name shall live from generation to generation.

Nations shall shew forth his wisdom, and the congregation shall declare his praise.

If he die, he shall leave a greater name than a thousand: and if he live, he shall increase it. (Ecclesiasticus 39: 1–11)

The book Ecclesiasticus was of more importance than we might sometimes suppose in the late Jewish and early Christian circles, and is the source of one of the most famous utterances recorded in St. Matthew's Gospel. I ask you to compare Matthew 11: 28–30:

Come to me all you who are weary and burdened and I will give you rest. Take my yoke upon you and learn from me, for I am gentle and humble in heart and you will find rest for your souls. For my yoke is easy and my burden is light.

and Ecclesiasticus 51: 23–26:

Drew near unto me, ye unlearned, and dwell in the house of learning. Wherefore are ye slow, and what say ye of these things, seeing your souls are very thirsty?

I opened my mouth, and said, Buy her for yourselves without money. Put your neck under the yoke, and let your soul receive instruction: she is hard at hand to find.

It is possible too, that Matthew 13: 52 is a modest reference to the author himself:

Every teacher of the law who has been instructed about the kingdom of heaven is like the owner of a house who brings out of his storeroom new treasures as well as old.

But these are minor points, suggestive no doubt, but

certainly not conclusive. His debt to the Old Testament is perhaps most clearly illustrated in the structure of his Gospel; it is divided into five sections marked by a similar recurrent phrase and intended, so many commentators believe, to suggest the five-fold construction of the Torah itself, the five books of Moses.[3] M.D. Goulder in his book *Midrash and Lection in Matthew* goes even further, and suggests that the whole Gospel is a midrash developed around his model, the Gospel according to St. Mark, without necessary recourse to any other sources.[4]

The word 'midrash' is a Jewish term derived from a word which means 'dig' and is applied to explanatory commentaries on the Old Testament. Not many scholars will go all the way with Goulder, but the fact that the suggestion can be made at all illustrates the depth and significance of Matthew's debt not only to the Old Testament, but to current Jewish attitudes to it. Matthew could indeed have seen himself as a 'scribe instructed in the kingdom of heaven who was bringing forth out of his treasures things new and old.' 'In his eyes he is the Christian inheritor of the noble title born by a line of servants of God from Ezra to Ben Sirach, and Hillel and Shammai.'[5]

Any discussion of Matthew's models leads on almost instinctively to the discussion of the fourth question listed above. What was his environment, physical, cultural and spiritual? I cannot do better than to begin this section with a quotation from Benedict Green's commentary on St. Matthew:[6]

It is widely agreed that it is to this stage in the emergence of Christianity from Judaism that Matthew belongs. In the first place he is dependent on Mark, which is now usually dated little if at all before A.D. 70, and time would be needed for it to become current in the Eastern Mediterranean. Secondly, Matthew not only makes Jesus refer bleakly to the fall of Jerusalem, and the destruction of the temple, but clearly

understands these events as a judgment on Israel for its
rejection of the Christ. He sees the future as lying not with a
revived Israel or a restored temple, but in a new community
founded on faith in Christ and recruited from the Gentile
world... we may regard Matthew as the work of a Jewish
Christian evangelist writing for a Greek speaking community
which lived probably outside Palestine in acute conflict with
the synagogue across the street.

This quotation draws attention once more to the
importance of the year A.D. 70 in the future development of
both Judaism and Christianity. We have seen already that
it could have been the fall of Jerusalem which provoked
the author of Matthew to set his hand to another Gospel.
But there is no doubt that the fall of Jerusalem drastically
changed the cultural and social environment which he
had previously occupied. Up to that time there had been
no hard and fast distinction between the ancient people of
God – the Jews – and the new people of God – the
Christians. No doubt families were divided by these
competing allegiances and there were tensions between
them which are vividly illustrated in the Acts of the
Apostles and the Pauline Epistles. But Christians living in
Jerusalem continued to worship in the temple and kept
the Sabbath and Jews were still prepared to honour one
whom many of them still regarded as a true teacher of the
Law and a descendant of David. The fall of Jerusalem
changed all that for ever. The temple was destroyed and
was never rebuilt. The Rabbinic establishment left
Jerusalem and for many years based itself in Jamnia.
Christians moved away into whatever village or city was
prepared to receive them and there was no longer the kind
of easy social intercourse which had previously characterised the relationships between them. Furthermore, the fall
of Jerusalem put Judaism on the defensive, anxious to
close ranks against any movement that would threaten the
survival or the integrity of Israel. The Christians now
came to be regarded not just as another sect within an

increasingly pluralistic Judaism but as an independent
body claiming for itself privileges which the Jewish
people had previously enjoyed. We do not know exactly
when the 'Separation' took place but it was certainly
under way in the communities to which Matthew
belonged and for which he wrote. If there is a new factor in
the 'environment' it must be this; it was this incipient
separation which called for a new Gospel and determined
its content and shape. I quote again from Benedict Green
in support of this view:

Everything changed drastically with the outcome of the
Jewish war and the destruction of Jerusalem in A.D. 70.
Sadducees, even if they had survived the conflict in any
considerable numbers, would have had no significant role in
the situation in which the temple had been destroyed; the
functions of the priesthood were generally in abeyance and
such native Jewish institutions as persisted were not based on
Jerusalem. The Pharisees, on the other hand, were not only
well adapted by their lack of commitment to the rebellion
against Rome and their relative unattachment to the temple
cultus to survive and take the lead in the reconstruction of
Judaism ... Jamnia certainly became in the years that followed
the real centre of the reconstruction of Jewish institutions in
Palestine, and the authoritative source of official Jewish
teaching.
    The only serious contenders with the Pharisees claiming to
represent true Judaism were the Christians. They too
remained uncompromised by the rebellion (the Christian
community of Jerusalem is credited with a withdrawal to Pella
in the Decapolis during the siege) and they were similarly free
of dependence on the temple. There is a certain amount of
indirect evidence both inside and outside the New Testament,
that Christians of this time were making a definite bid for
recognition by the outside world as the true successors of the
old Israel.[7]

If we now address ourselves to the last of the questions
with which this chapter began we shall have to say that it

was the environment which provided Matthew with the main theological and practical questions which are treated in his Gospel.

What did Matthew have in mind when he sat down in front of St. Mark's Gospel, and whom did he have in mind? This calls for an exercise of imagination rather than just for academic expertise, and in suggesting this I take comfort from G.H. Morrison's words:[8]

> He sees by the gift of a trained imagination into the heart of men and the character of movements. And though he may lack the minute and critical knowledge that is in the keeping of laborious students, yet he often brings us nearer to the truth than the man who discovers and refutes his errors.

As we have seen already, the fall of Jerusalem created problems and tensions which had scarcely been felt with the same intensity before. I ask you to imagine the situation of the scribe described in St. Mark 12: 28-34:

> One of the teachers of the law came and heard them debating. Noticing that Jesus had given them a good answer, he asked him, 'Of all the commandments, which is the most important?'
>
> 'The most important one,' answered Jesus, 'is this, "Hear, O Israel, the Lord our God, the Lord is one. Love the Lord your God with all your heart and with all your soul and with all your mind and with all your strength." The second is this: "Love your neighbour as yourself." There is no commandment greater than these.'
>
> 'Well said, teacher,' the man replied. 'You are right in saying that God is one and there is no other but him. To love him with all your heart, with all your understanding and with all your strength, and to love your neighbour as yourself is more important than all burnt offerings and sacrifices.'
>
> When Jesus saw that he had answered wisely, he said to him, 'You are not far from the kingdom of God.' And from then on no-one dared ask him any more questions.

This passage may well have been preserved in Mark's

tradition because as in some other cases in the Gospel the person in question may ultimately have heard the Gospel and had become a member of the Church.[9] He had been a scribe, a fervent follower of Moses, a pillar of orthodoxy and an enthusiast for the law. Supposing him to have been young when he first encountered Jesus, supposing also that he had survived the fall of Jerusalem, he would find himself now in an extremely painful position. When Christians and Jews had 'cohabited' in Jerusalem and in the villages and towns of Judea it would not have been impossible for him to be a believer in Christ and continue his office as a scribe. He would have felt, of course, the cold blasts of controversy created by the Pauline mission to the Gentiles, but he would not have been excluded from the synagogue by virtue of his new-found faith. He would have been regarded as a somewhat eccentric representative of the scribal party, but still a representative of it. In the earliest days of the Methodist movement, there were many Anglican clergy who had to live with their membership of the Church of England and with their enthusiasm for Wesley's mission. He would have continued to observe the Jewish law with regard to fasting, ritual uncleanness, the observance of the Sabbath. There would not have been much occasion anyway for eating with Gentiles. This was not an heroic stance, but on the other hand, Peter and even Paul permitted themselves on occasion compromises of this kind. He would have attended the synagogue on Saturday, and even instructed the faithful there, and on Sunday morning he could have been one of a group gathered round the table of the Lord and singing hymns to Christ. There are after all Messianic groups of this kind in existence in Israel today and there is no necessary contradiction given the fact that Jesus had been a Jew Himself, had been an honoured teacher of the Law and was certainly regarded by many of his compatriots as, if nothing more, a Prophet of Israel.

But now I ask you to imagine the situation after the fall of Jerusalem. This comfortable 'compromise' was no longer possible because our scribe now found himself in a much more conspicuous situation as a member of a Christian community in, say, one of the towns or villages of Galilee, which increasingly came to be regarded as heretical. The practising Jews of the community would not take kindly to having in their midst a previous member of their order who was a member of a sect which threatened the unity and integrity of Israel at a time of alarming crisis in Jewish affairs. Furthermore, the scribal order did not owe allegiance simply to the local synagogue but increasingly to a Jewish authority now centralised in Jamnia. The battle lines were drawn and Jews and Christians manned the barricades across many a street in many a Jewish town. We shall assume that our scribe who had not been far from the kingdom of God would not now disown the Christ, but you can sympathise with his feelings when he manned the barricade on the side of the Christians when the other side was manned by his own peers, his own associates within the ancient religion of Judah. Not only would he have personal misgivings about the decision he was compelled to make (Jews who subsequently have made that journey from Judaism to Christianity can vouch for that) but he will have to face certain inescapable dilemmas arising out of his new situation. For example, what is he to do now about the practical obligations of his old religion? Should he still observe the dietary regulations, should he accept the normal purification ceremonies, should he continue to fast? And he could hardly man the barricades on Friday and attend the synagogue service on Saturday. It is highly unlikely that he would have been accepted in the synagogue anyway. Benedict Green refers in his commentary to this situation:[10]

Bitter hostility towards Christianity from now on characterises Rabbinic writings and culminated historically in the addition around A.D. 85 of the so-called 'Test Benediction', the prayer of eighteen Benedictions recited daily in the synagogue. This ran 'let Christians and Minim (heretics) perish in a moment, let them be blotted out of the book of the living and let them not be written with the righteous.' No Christians could say Amen to this or remain in the synagogue while it was recited. The inevitable and intended result was the exclusion of Christians from synagogues everywhere. In areas of mixed population this must have led to a large accession of Jewish Christians to the already separate churches of the Gentiles; in Palestine wherever Jamnia was in effective control it can only have meant the reduction of the Christians to a hated, if not actually persecutèd, minority.

This view is challenged in detail by Reuven Kinelman[11] but the fact that Christians were persecuted by their Jewish countrymen is not seriously in doubt. The Acts of the Apostles reflects an early stage in the hostilities between Jews and Christians and the fall of Jerusalem would certainly have aggravated the situation.

But if our scribe had practical problems which cried out for resolution, he also had his intellectual, moral and spiritual problems. Convinced as he was that Jesus of Nazareth was the true Messiah predicted by the prophets, what is he to make of the fact that Jewish religious establishments by and large have rejected him? Not only did this undoubtedly fuel the inevitable misgivings which such a man as this would have felt about alienation from his past and from his peers, but it raised acute problems about the present status of people of God who had rejected, it would seem, the man whom God had sent them. Did he have to believe that exclusive privileges of the Hebrews had been abrogated forever? Did all their sufferings from the time of Moses down to the present day count for nothing? Did all this history, faith and longing, sacrifice and self-denial reach its end term at the foot of a cross on a little hill just outside Jerusalem where Jesus was cruelly and in his view unjustly crucified?

These problems troubled the mind of a greater man,

Paul of Tarsus, who had preceded our scribe on this painful journey of self-doubt. But at least Paul had had his vision to sustain him in these times of doubt; he had ranged the world experiencing the effects of the preaching of the Gospel far and wide from Antioch to Rome. But our scribe was a member of a small Christian community now ranged against the ancient religion out of which it was born. He was being asked to believe that the privileges attaching to the ancient people of God had now been inherited by these little, vulnerable Christian communities, to one of which the scribe belonged. This calls for an over-view of history to which few of us indeed can possibly aspire, and it would have been another factor causing confusions of heart and mind for many converts from Judaism to Christianity. But perhaps the most serious problem our scribe would encounter would be the moral and spiritual one. Here was a man who had lived by the rules of his religion, believing that faithful observance of the rules would assure him God's favour on earth and in heaven. It had been a demanding life imposing endless vigilance upon the man who attempted it, but it had its satisfactions – the satisfaction of living by Law, the satisfaction of a fast well kept, of a temptation resisted, the satisfaction of walking in a known way towards a known objective. There had been difficulties of course; it was not always easy to establish the right priorities; one commandment might seem to run counter to another in determining a course of action, and it is evident from various encounters recorded in the Gospels that there were some in the religious establishment of the day who felt profoundly unsatisfied with the way of life which was prescribed. So the scribe referred to in the passage already quoted from St. Mark was no doubt echoing a familiar question in first-century Judaism – amidst all the rules and regulations and precepts and counsels, 'what is the first commandment of all?' He had assented to Jesus' answer and had thereby won for himself that word of praise and encouragement – 'you are not far from the Kingdom of God.' But our scribe now had to take on board the position articulated by St. Paul in the very earliest days of the Church. Salvation was not just to be achieved by however rigorous attention to the rules and regulations of the Torah, but by faith in Christ. He had believed and had thereby been saved, but if he had been delivered from the rule of Law what was there now to put in its place? 'Love the Lord your God and your neighbour as yourself' Jesus had said – a large commandment but not all that easy to apply to the inner life of a believer or to his outward conduct in the world. Our scribe might well have found himself thinking if not saying, 'me this unchartered freedom tires; I feel the weight of chance desires.' Could it be that Matthew himself had faced this dilemma in his own life and was concerned in his Gospel to minister to Jewish Christians everywhere who were looking for a way of life consonant with their profession yet without the Torah upon which they had once relied? This could be the reason why Matthew chose to construct his work in five sections corresponding to the ancient Torah. The Torah had ceased to be a way of salvation, but there was a new Torah available to those who were already in the way of salvation through Christ. In this new Torah, the Sermon on the Mount takes pride of place, and perhaps Dr. Sandmel is right when he suggests that 'the Sermon on the Mount is the clue to the significance of the entire Gospel.'[12]

Perhaps we ought to give Dr. Sandmel the last word in this chapter. Himself a Jewish scholar of wide repute known for his knowledge of and sympathy towards Christian scholarship, hear what he has to say about the Gospel we have been studying together in this chapter:

Matthew's portrayal of Jesus as a new Moses who did not come to abolish the Law and the Prophets is not to be viewed or designed to validate or revalidate the Laws of Moses or to establish or re-establish prophetic authority. The intent is to give a prelude to a brand new Law, a Christian Law, obedience to which is to effect a righteousness which is to surpass that of scribes and Pharisees. Hence it is not the Mosaic law or the Hebrew prophets here being commended but rather Matthew's version of Christianity.[13]

I hasten to add that this has been an exercise in imagination not in exact scholarship. No such scribe may have existed but the conditions of the latter part of the first century certainly did exist in Palestine and elsewhere. Read Matthew's Gospel as a whole and you will see how these conditions have affected not only the shape but the content of his Gospel. This could have been what he had in mind when he sat down in front of his version of St. Mark's Gospel and contemplated the work which lay ahead of him. It remains a Gospel 'according to St. Matthew', and for the purposes of this particular book we have to understand Matthew's particular attitude towards his subject, if we are to handle with any success that great comprehensive view of life enshrined in the Sermon on the Mount and in those mysterious 'Beatitudes'.

## Chapter 3

# THE SERMON ON THE MOUNT

As a parish priest I have had it said to me on more than one occasion that we do not need the Church or the complicated dogmas with which the Church is sometimes associated; all we need to do is to live by the Sermon on the Mount. 'All we need to do . . .' Even the title 'Sermon on the Mount' raises many questions, as we shall see, and many of the sayings incorporated in it are not only difficult to interpret but impracticable in terms of everyday life. I quote just a few of them as an example of the demands which are being made by this 'simple' Sermon on the Mount:

> You have heard that it was said, 'Do not commit adultery'. But I tell you that anyone who looks at a woman lustfully has already committed adultery with her in his heart. (Matthew 5: 27-28)
>
> You have heard that it was said, 'Eye for eye, and tooth for tooth.' But I tell you, Do not resist an evil person. If someone strikes you on the right cheek, turn to him the other also. And if someone wants to sue you and take your tunic, let him have your cloak as well. (Matthew 5: 38-40)
>
> So do not worry, saying, 'What shall we eat?' or 'What shall we drink?' or 'What shall we wear?' For the pagans run after all these things, and your heavenly Father knows that you need them. But seek first his kingdom and his righteousness, and all these things will be given to you as well. Therefore do not worry about tomorrow, for tomorrow will worry about itself.

Each day has enough trouble of its own. (Matthew 6: 31-34)
    Ask and it will be given to you; seek and you will find; knock
and the door will be opened to you. For everyone who asks
receives; he who seeks finds; and to him who knocks, the door
will be opened. (Matthew 7: 7-8)

Could my friend have looked me in the eye and said that
his daily life was consonant with such teaching? But most
of my readers will not need to be convinced. The Sermon
calls for a kind of sacrificial life which for most of us seems
way beyond the range of individual or social possibilities.
Taken seriously these sayings are like the thunder and
lightning of Sinai, destroying all human pretensions,
laying the soul naked before the eyes of Him with whom
we have to do. There is no way as far as my experience goes
of 'living by the Sermon on the Mount'. There have been
times in my own life when I have been stabbed alive by
these uncompromising sayings and have felt like the
people of Israel who 'saw the thunderings and the
lightnings and the voice of the trumpet, and the mountain
smoking: and . . . trembled and stood afar off' (Exodus 20:
18, R.V.). However, it is unlikely that the Beatitudes can be
meaningful if we do not consider the Sermon of which
they are supposed to be part. The literature on the subject
is voluminous, but much of it quite inaccessible to the
ordinary reader or even to the amateur scholar. The fact
that this enormous literature exists is a witness to both the
complexity and the importance of the subject we now have
in hand.
Ways of looking at the Sermon on the Mount have
varied from century to century and have of course been
conditioned by the cultural environment to which each
interpreter belongs. The Sermon meant one thing to St.
Augustine of Hippo and quite another to Karl Marx. It
means one thing to a well-endowed capitalist society; it
means something rather different to a poorer member of a
Third-World country. I have, however, for the purposes of

simplicity isolated five possible attitudes to it, each of which has commanded at some time or in some place a substantial body of scholarly support. The first is what Jeremias calls the 'perfectionist conception'.

'In the Sermon on the Mount Jesus tells his disciples what he requires of them. He unfolds for them the will of God as this should determine their way of life.'[1] It is not entirely due to the hardness of our hearts that most of us find this 'perfectionist conception' impossible. There is after all a genuine theological question as to whether it is possible to reconcile such a view with the Pauline view of the inherent sinfulness of human nature and our unceasing dependence on God for salvation and grace. If the Christian life is seen as a life of explicit obedience to moral precepts, are we in any better case than our Jewish ancestors in the faith who saw their own ideal way of life in precisely these terms? Closely associated with this attitude is a second one which acknowledges the radical and uncompromising nature of the Sermon on the Mount and in a sense turns it on its head by treating it as an impossible ideal intended to engender in us a sense of despair which will itself lead to repentance, forgiveness and new life. So the new sermon from the mountain in Galilee is like the old sermon from the mountain of Sinai, a tutor intended to lead us to Christ.[2] That the Sermon has fulfilled such a function no one would deny. That it was uttered for this purpose seems to me and to many others unlikely. The position is stated paradoxically in Robert Frost's 'Mask of Mercy' quoted by Harvey MacArthur in his *Understanding the Sermon on the Mount*[3]:

> The Sermon on the Mount
> Is just a frame-up to ensure the failure
> Of all of us so all of us will be
> Thrown prostrate at the mercy seat for mercy.

A third possibility, often canvassed, is that the Sermon on

the Mount is the description of a future state in a world utterly transformed from the world in which we live, freed from the restraints and ambition, the bitterness and the greed which characterise the world as we know it now. This view is not to be dismissed out of hand as an easy escape from the demands of the Sermon here and now, because it does have some precedent in Scripture itself. The prophet Isaiah, using highly symbolic language, looks forward to such a day here on earth when

> the wolf shall dwell with the lamb, and the leopard shall lie down with the kid; and the calf and the young lion and the fatling together; and a little child shall lead them. And the cow and the bear shall feed; their young ones shall lie down together; and the lion shall eat straw like the ox. And the sucking child shall play on the hole of the asp, and the weaned child shall put his hand on the basilisk's den. They shall not hurt nor destroy in all my holy mountain: for the earth shall be full of the knowledge of the Lord, as the waters cover the sea. (Isaiah 11: 6-9, R.V.).

The author of the Book of Revelation, not all that distant in time or even place from the author of St. Matthew's Gospel, likewise envisaged the coming perfect state on earth:

> Then I saw a new heaven and a new earth, for the first heaven and the first earth had passed away, and there was no longer any sea. I saw the Holy City, the new Jerusalem, coming down out of heaven from God, prepared as a bride beautifully dressed for her husband. And I heard a loud voice from the throne saying, 'Now the dwelling of God is with men, and he will live with them. They will be his people, and God himself will be with them and be their God. He will wipe every tear from their eyes. There will be no more death or mourning or crying or pain, for the old order of things has passed away.'
>
> He who was seated on the throne said, 'I am making everything new!' Then he said, 'Write this down, for these words are trustworthy and true.'

He said to me: 'It is done. I am the Alpha and the Omega, the Beginning and the End. To him who is thirsty I will give to drink without cost from the spring of the water of life. He who overcomes will inherit all this, and I will be his God and he will be my son. But the cowardly, the unbelieving, the vile, the murderers, the sexually immoral, those who practise magic arts, the idolaters and all liars – their place will be in the fiery lake of burning sulphur. This is the second death.' (Revelation 21: 1–8)

There is no doubt that the early Christians of Matthew's day were animated by just such visions of the future. But there is no indication in the text itself that the Sermon on the Mount was intended to be interpreted in this way but as commandments and precepts for the here and now, for today and tomorrow, for communal life in Capernaum or Nazareth or, for that matter, in Ephesus or Philippi.

The fourth possibility we might describe as 'the way of salvation' understood in the following sense:

The main-stream of the Christian tradition merged the Sermon with the Pauline insistence on salvation by grace by asserting that the demands of the Sermon could be fulfilled only by those who had already received the spirit of God by grace through faith. That is, the Sermon was understood not so much as a gateway to God but rather as the path to be followed by those who had already gone through the gate. It was a guide for those within the Kingdom (in this context the Church) rather than the road into that Kingdom.[4]

The virtue of this particular view is that it more nearly corresponds to actual experience. My friend who thought it was possible to live by the Sermon on the Mount without entangling himself with the Church or professing the faith would soon have discovered how vain was his hope. But he would have discovered too, had he yielded his life to Christ, that in hidden and mysterious ways grace could achieve what unaided human nature never could have achieved. This view of the Sermon on the Mount makes it no less demanding but opens up the possibility that here and there, by degrees, imperfectly but hopefully, a Christian man might begin to find himself living this way, 'the way of salvation'.

But perhaps the most familiar theory to those of us who have passed through the theological schools over the past forty years has been the theory called 'the interim ethic'. It depends on a view not inaugurated but certainly popularised by Schweitzer[5] that the whole of first-century Christianity was dominated by the often-expressed conviction of our Lord Himself that He would return in the lifetime of His apostles. This conviction is reflected in the very earliest records of the church, e.g. Mark 9: 1:

> And he said to them, 'I tell you the truth, some who are standing here will not taste death before they see the kingdom of God come with power.'

In Schweitzer's view the whole of the early Church lived in a ferment of excited expectation in which all the normal conditions of human life were held to be in abeyance and the Christian's chief occupation was to 'watch' for the return of his master. If this is so, then the Sermon belongs to this particular stage in the Church's history where it was indeed possible for little Christian communities to live by the precepts of the Sermon without having to face the problems inherent in the wider application of these precepts to the world as a whole.

No one would doubt the importance of Schweitzer's view. It profoundly influenced the world of scholarship even if now it has few wholehearted supporters. Perhaps the most serious objection to it is that there is every likelihood that St. Matthew's Gospel saw the light of day in its entirety after the fall of Jerusalem in A.D. 70 at a time when the Church, which had (wrongly as it proved) assumed that the fall of Jerusalem would herald the end of the world, was having to come to terms with a rather longer view of its role in history. The Sermon on the Mount suggests not so much an interim ethic intended for twenty or thirty excited years, as a systematic attempt to help Christians individually and corporately along a hard way; it was intended, shall we say, for pilgrims on the road rather than for watchmen in the tower. If we are to achieve any persuasive view of the Sermon we have to take seriously the mind of the author of St. Matthew's Gospel and conditions in the Church and in society generally to which his Gospel is addressed. This is the point, therefore, at which we have to refer back to the previous chapter and ask whether the conclusions to which we were led concerning the nature and circumstances of the author of the Gospel have something to say to us about the nature and purpose of the Sermon which comprises a substantial part of it.

The Gospel, so we have argued, arose and reached its final form in a period of growing estrangement between Judaism and Christianity. This is put as well as it is possible to put it in the words of Dr. W.D. Davies:[6]

> The shattering of the Jewish State made possible the emergence of the Pharisaic party, which had hitherto only been one among many others, as the leading force in Judaism. Under the initial leadership of Rabbi Johannan Ben Zakkai, it was the Pharisees of Jamnia who laid the foundations for the more concentrated and homogeneous Rabbinic Judaism of later history. It is therefore difficult to exaggerate the significance for Jewish history of the events that followed the fall of the city. But strangely enough their possible relevance for the life of the Christian church has been little exploited, and it will now be our task to ask whether Matthew, and the Sermon on the Mount in particular, owe anything to the impact of what we shall call the Jamnian Period.

The question is precisely put but as one would expect, given all the uncertainties concerning the relationship between Jews and Christians in the first century, less precisely answered. However, Dr. Davies does permit himself the view that 'the Sermon on the Mount is illumined when understood in terms of the enthusiasm of a Galilean movement over against the realism of the Jamnian.'[7] On the one hand you have an embattled Judaism striving for unity, extirpating heresy, codifying its rules and regulations, looking for a new identity in a shattered world. On the other hand, you have an enthusiastic movement arising out of Judaism but at odds with it, enthusiastic, growing rapidly, confident that its members had inherited the privileges and responsibilities of the ancient people of God. The fact that Matthew divides his book into five parts corresponding to the five books of Moses, and that he locates the delivery of the Sermon on a mountain, suggests that Matthew is privy to the problems experienced by our imaginary scribe and wishes to offer him a new Moses, a new Law and a new community within which to live out his new life. I can think of no greater service that Matthew could have done for those early Christians grieved at heart at the rejection of the Messiah by their own people and at a loss to understand the implications of that rejection for their own life and witness. It is unlikely that such a view of the Sermon on the Mount will explain every feature in it or answer every question arising from it, but it does provide a view which is at least consonant with much that we do know about the life of the Church in the last decades of the first century. Any exegesis which wholly ignores what we might call 'the setting of the Sermon on the Mount' can hardly do justice to the oracles and sayings which comprise it.

But we cannot of course be content with the 'setting of the Sermon on the Mount' if we think of the setting only in terms of the early history of the Church. We have at least to consider the setting of the Sermon on the Mount fifty years earlier when the multitudes from Galilee and Decapolis and Jerusalem and Judaea and from beyond Jordan[8] saw

Jesus of Nazareth withdrawing to the mountain and calling His disciples to Him. We have at least to consider what those 'disciples' thought of these strange paradoxical utterances, how they reacted to this new teacher of the Law as He outlined the way of salvation and blessedness. What did the sermon mean to them as their hearts were lifted and their minds challenged by the words and works of this young prophet from Nazareth?

First of all, however, we have to ask whether there ever was such a 'Sermon' at all. Chapters 5 to 7 which constitute the Sermon in St. Matthew's Gospel, even when read with judicious pauses, will take less than twenty minutes. That may be a statutory time for an Anglican sermon but it was not the way of the Rabbis. It was a commonplace of Jewish life that eager disciples would attach themselves to a favoured Rabbi, live with him, share his table and absorb his teaching. Their instruction was not a sermon in our sense of that word within the confines of an ecclesiastical building and a formal liturgy. Rabbinic teaching was not without its Socratic models and we have some understanding how it was conducted. Dr. Daube in his book offers several examples of the ways in which public and private discourses were conducted by the Rabbinic teachers of the day. A discourse could be sparked off by an encounter in public with a rival Rabbi. Then there follows a deceptively simple, gnomic utterance intended to provoke or to silence his rival, and then in private with his own disciples the Rabbi expounds the exchange at greater length.[9] Thus teaching and circumstance were closely integrated, and the discourse which results may lack any obvious shape and indeed be largely incomprehensible unless we can know or at least hazard a guess at the circumstance which provoked it.

Even, therefore, if the Sermon on the Mount is to be seen as one discourse given at one time in one place we shall have to imagine it greatly enlarged and much less formalised than we have it in the Gospel, given not in the matter of twenty minutes but in a period of several days. Even given the phenomenal memory which characterises the Semitic races as a whole and the memory training exercises to which a Jewish child was exposed, it would be difficult to imagine that such a discursive sermon could be wholly remembered and infallibly transmitted. I would not myself exclude the possibility that the Sermon as we have it is a resumé, preserved in the tradition, of an extended period of teaching given more or less in one place and on one occasion. However, it is perhaps more likely that Matthew himself was responsible for gathering the material from various sources in the church of his day which had been preserved in oral or written form and had already been used as part of the staple diet of the early Christian communities learning to walk in the way of salvation. Perhaps we do not have to decide between those two options and that is just as well because I see no way in which conclusive evidence for either can be produced. Either way, we have to ask whether the Sermon conforms to a perceptible structure, whether it can be analysed and yield a consistent message, whether its constituent parts make up a whole and whether it offers us now as it apparently did in Matthew's day a reliable and comprehensive guide for those who wish to walk in the way of salvation.

Every writer on the Sermon on the Mount feels under obligation to provide some kind of analysis and thereby assumes that in the mind of Jesus Himself or in the mind of Matthew it constituted a coherent whole and a developing argument. Of course, we may be wrong. Perhaps we would be wiser to describe the Sermon on the Mount as 'the sayings of Jesus' on a par with the sayings of Mao or the sayings of Confucius or the sayings of the Buddha or 'the tales of the Hasidim'.[10] As such they would remain an invaluable guide to the life and teaching of Jesus and an all-important contribution to our understanding of the religious life. But we must not give in so

easily. Perhaps this is a sermon with a beginning, three
points and an end, which encapsulates the essential
teaching of Christ for those who are His disciples and wish
to follow Him in the way. The 'extra volume' of Hastings'
*Dictionary of the Bible*[11] provides a learned and exhaustive
article on the Sermon on the Mount and offers the
following simple analysis:

A) The ideal life described
   a) Its characteristics
   b) Its mission
B) Its relation to the earlier Hebrew ideal
C) The outworkings of the ideal life
   a) In deeds and motives
   b) In real religious worship
   c) In trust and self-devotion
   d) In treatment of others
D) The duty of living the ideal life.

That remains a good working analysis and at least the
theme is clear – the Sermon on the Mount is concerned
with the ideal life. I offer just one other, more recent
example of a very different type of analysis, which assumes
the unity of the Sermon (either in the mind of Our Lord or
in the mind of Matthew) but on wholly different
grounds:[12]

### THE UNITY OF THE SERMON

Beatitudes

| | | |
|---|---|---|
| (8) Persecuted | (a) Reward in heaven | 5: 11–12 |
| | (b) Salt of earth | 5: 13 |
| | (c) Light of cosmos | 5: 14–16 |
| | Law and Prophets fulfilled | |
| (7) Peacemakers | (a) No anger, rudeness, insult | 5: 21–2 |
| | (b) Reconciliation | 5: 23–4 |
| | (c) Come to terms | 5: 25–6 |
| (6) Pure in heart | (a) No lust (heart/eyes/hands) | 5: 27–30 |
| | (b) No remarriage | 5: 31–2 |
| | (c) No false oaths (Ps. 24: 4) | 5: 33–7 |

| (5) Merciful | (a) No *talio* | 5: 38–42 |
| | (b) No hatred | 5: 43–8 |
| | (c) No parade in 'mercy' | 6: 1–4 |
| (4) Hunger and | (a) No parade in prayer | 6: 5–8 |
| thirst for | (b) Lord's Prayer | 6: 9–15 |
| righteousness | (c) No parade in fasting | 6: 16–18 |
| (3) Meek | (a) Treasure in heaven | 6: 19–21 |
| (Ps. 37: 11) | (b) Generous eye | 6: 22–4 |
| | (c) No anxiety | 6: 25–34 |
| (2) Mourners | (a) No judging | 7: 1–2 |
| | (b) No reproving | 7: 3–5 |
| | (c) No backbiting | 7: 6 |
| (1) Poor in | Ask, seek, knock | 7: 7–11 |
| spirit | Law and Prophets in a Kelal | 7: 12 |
| Peroration | (a) Two Gates, Two Ways | 7: 13–14 |
| | (b) False prophets, Two Trees and Fruits | 7: 15–23 |
| | (c) Two Builders | 7: 24–7 |

I would ask you to look carefully at Dr. Goulder's analysis because you will observe that whole discourse hinges on the Beatitudes which stand at the beginning of it. Dr. Goulder presses this interpretation with varying success but at least it is not inherently unlikely. If the Rabbinic sermon sometimes started with a gnomic utterance, subsequently elaborated and illustrated in discussion with disciples, then at least we do have a model on which it is possible, though never easy, to attempt an interpretation of the parts in the context of the whole. Even if the analysis is wrong in detail it makes it possible for us to believe that the Beatitudes are integral to the Sermon and the Sermon integral to the Beatitudes – and this is no small gain in interpreting both. At least our imaginary scribe with the Sermon in his hand would have felt at home with the method.

I end this chapter with Dr. Sandmel's considered view of the matter:[13]

The Sermon on the Mount is the clue to the significance of the entire Gospel. Mark is essentially a negative writing in the sense that Mark instructs Christians about what to avoid, not about what to do. The opposite is the case with Matthew. He provides affirmative instructions which tell the faithful what they are to do in a range of situations whether prayer, the giving of alms or the dealing with fellow human beings. The Sermon on the Mount provides guidance, that is, it gives the answer to the implied question – what is the proper Christian life?

# Chapter 4

# BEATITUDES

The Bible was not written in Tudor English and Jesus did not speak in Tudor English. It is a mark of our devotion to the King James' version of the Bible that it is necessary to make this obvious remark. That particular version and for that matter any English version of the Bible is a translation which stands at the end of a long process of transmission. The language of the Old Testament is Hebrew with small sections of it in Aramaic. The language of the New Testament is Greek with a few Aramaic words embedded in it. It is certain that Our Lord did not speak in Tudor English but that is the only fact about which we can be absolutely certain. The presumption is that for the greater part He spoke in Aramaic. Aramaic was a Semitic language which had long been spoken by the Aramaeans in Northern Syria and Mesopotamia and had become the chief language for commercial and diplomatic transactions. As I have said, it has its place in the Old Testament itself, e.g. in Ezra and Daniel. It is one of the conundrums of Old Testament scholarship why one large section of the Book of Daniel 2: 4 to 7: 28, should have been written in Aramaic when the first and last sections of the book are written in Hebrew. I will not burden you with possible explanations. I refer to it only to make the point that Aramaic had achieved such currency in the centuries preceding Christ that it had won its way even into the sacred Scriptures of the Hebrew people. Persuasive arguments have been put forward for the theory that some sections of the New Testament also were originally written in Aramaic and only subsequently translated into Greek.

In the world in which Jesus lived and taught, 'classical Hebrew', if we may call it such, had become the language of the learned, and the synagogue readings themselves had to be accompanied by a translation in Aramaic if the congregation were to understand them. The name given to such translations is 'Targum'. We have to assume therefore that Our Lord's public teaching was given in the language understood by the majority of the people whom He addressed. An early example of this teaching is to be found in St. Luke's account of Jesus' first 'sermon' in the synagogue in Nazareth:

> He went to Nazareth, where he had been brought up, and on the Sabbath day he went into the synagogue, as was his custom. And he stood up to read. The scroll of the prophet Isaiah was handed to him. Unrolling it, he found the place where it is written:
> 'The Spirit of the Lord is on me,
> because he has anointed me
> to preach good news to the poor.
> He has sent me to proclaim freedom for the prisoners
> and recovery of sight for the blind,
> to release the oppressed,
> to proclaim the year of the Lord's favour.'
> Then he rolled up the scroll, gave it back to the attendant and sat down. The eyes of everyone in the synagogue were fastened on him, and he began by saying to them, 'Today this scripture is fulfilled in your hearing.' (Luke 4: 16–21)

It seems that Jesus was familiar enough with ancient Hebrew to be able to read from the Hebrew Scriptures, because otherwise He would not have been invited to take a public part in the synagogue service. It is possible, though given the abbreviated report in Luke difficult to prove, that Jesus not only read the original Hebrew

Scripture but translated and interpreted it as well.[1] If Jesus was, as I have suggested elsewhere, an authentic even if irregular Rabbi, it seems certain that He was acquainted with Hebrew. The second question is whether in addition to Aramaic and Hebrew He also spoke Greek.

Alexander the Great had been not only a great military conqueror; he had been an enthusiast for Greek culture. In the cities of the Near East which he conquered or created he and his successors assiduously cultivated the use of the Greek language and the dissemination of Greek literature. In every major city they sought to establish a Greek academy, to create a gymnasium to mount Olympic-type games and to establish theatres for the production of Greek drama. It was one of the great problems of the Jews, a relatively small ethnic group scattered all over the Alexandrian empire, as to how far they could come to terms with this alien creature and how far they must protect themselves from it if they were to be faithful to their own traditions.[2] It was one of the most difficult and persistent problems which the Jewish people ever had to face. It created divisions in the ghetto and even in the family. In the end, some compromise was inevitable if Jews were to be able to conduct business in the world and relate to their Greek neighbours. So, Jesus lived, Dr. Mussies says:

> in a linguistic territory, if we may so call the remaining Jewish country, which was so strongly fragmented and had so many enclaves that knowledge of Greek must have been much more widely spread than the mere presence of some Greek schools and synagogues in Jerusalem might suggest. The New Testament and other testimonies point in the same direction. Moreover, the language of the aristocracy and the Roman government was Greek. Even one of the very last survivors of the revolt, a Judas in Masada, receives a letter in Greek about such an ordinary affair as the supply of vegetables. On the other hand, we must take care not to exaggerate: Greek remained a second language to the people at large.[3]

So, did Jesus speak Greek? Such evidence as we have in the New Testament suggests that He did. The conversations between Jesus and the Centurion, between Jesus and Pilate, between Peter and Cornelius all give the impression of having taken place without an interpreter and this view is reinforced by Dr. Argyle in a useful article in the *Expository Times*, Volume 67, from which I quote:

> Jesus was brought up in Galilee where many of the inhabitants would be Greek-speaking Gentiles. If he held intercourse with these, conducted a carpenter's business of which many of these would be customers, and preached to multitudes of them, he must have spoken Greek. So must Peter and Andrew, James and John, if they sold their fish to Gentile markets, and so must Levi being engaged in government employ. If Jesus in his teaching alluded to the Septuagint (that is the Greek version of the Old Testament) even where it differed from the Hebrew, he must have known Greek.[4]

I have engaged on this seeming digression on the languages of Palestine to make the reader aware of how far the words of Christ have travelled before they reached the pages of the King James' version and acquired the rich associations of Tudor English in the English mind. The Beatitudes themselves for all their seeming simplicity have a long linguistic history if, as we must suppose from the argument of this chapter, they were originally uttered in Aramaic, they carried overtones from the Hebrew of the Old Testament and were subsequently translated into Greek for the benefit of the members of the early Church, most of whom did not know Hebrew and many of whom did not know Aramaic either. The exposition of the Beatitudes in the second part of this book will have to have taken account of this long and often uncertain linguistic process. There is, if I may say so at this point, nothing simple about the 'simple Beatitudes'.

The omission of the definite article from the title of this chapter is deliberate. We take for granted that when we

speak of the Beatitudes we are speaking of those pregnant
sayings contained in Matthew's Gospel, Chapter 5, verses
1 to 12 and part of the Sermon on the Mount. But the
formula 'blessed are . . .' is not confined to Matthew 5 to 7
and is to be found elsewhere in the New Testament as the
following quotations show:

> Blessed is he who shall find no occasion of stumbling in me.
> Blessed is the man who does not fall away on account of me.
> Blessed are your eyes for they see and your ears for they hear.
> Blessed are you, Simon son of Jonah, for this was not revealed
> to you by man, but by my Father in heaven.
> Blessed are they that hear the word of God and keep it.
> Blessed are those servants whose master finds them watching
> when he comes.
> If you know these things, blessed are you if you do them.
> Blessed are they that have not seen and yet have believed.

The formula is also found in the Book of Revelation 1: 3,
14: 13, 16: 15, 19: 9, 22: 7. It is to be found in the Old
Testament and notably in the Psalms where it occurs at
least eighteen times. Perhaps even more significantly from
the point of view of Matthew, a group of Beatitudes occurs
in Ecclesiasticus 25: 7–10, where the English translation
offers 'happy' instead of 'blessed'.

> There be nine things that I have thought of and in mine heart
> counted happy,
> And the tenth I will utter with my tongue:
> A man that hath joy of his children;
> A man that liveth and looketh upon the fall of his enemies:
> Happy is he that dwelleth with a wife of understanding;
> And he that hath not slipped with his tongue;
> And he that hath not served a man that is unworthy of him;
> Happy is he that hath found prudence;
> And he that discourseth in the ears of them that listen.
> How great is he that has found wisdom.
> Yet is there none above him that feareth the Lord.
> The fear of the Lord passeth all things:
> He that holdeth it, to whom shall he be likened? (R.V.)

It seems to be unlikely that Matthew would have been entirely unaffected by a literary form so prominent already in the Scripture of his people. And it seems to me likely that the passage quoted above from Ecclesiasticus, the work of a revered scribe, affected his arrangement of the 'Beatitudes'. But we must then go on to ask what principle of selection was at work in Matthew's mind given the fact that there are three other 'Beatitudes' in his own Gospel and that Luke has made a different selection at the beginning of his 'Sermon on the Plain' (Luke 6: 20-23).

We must however go further back still, and ask which of the versions of the Beatitudes in Matthew and Luke corresponds most nearly to the actual words of Christ in the Sermon on the Mount. If Matthew and Luke had in front of them the same traditional material, why did Matthew record nine and Luke only four? Or were there only four in the original which Luke quoted faithfully, but to which Matthew assimilated five more from elsewhere in the tradition known to him? And of course we cannot be quite sure, despite Dr. Goulder's powerful advocacy, that the Beatitudes are in any case part of the original discourse. To these questions I have to say that there is no generally agreed answer, and the reader will have to be content with the answers implied by the exposition of the Beatitudes in the second part of this book. A lot will depend upon your view of the purpose of Matthew's Gospel as a whole. If Matthew was a member of the scribal class (if I may use that loose expression) and was writing for people with a similar background and with similar problems, he would have been at pains as far as possible to relate the new Torah of Christ to the old Torah of Moses. He would not need to press comparisons between Christ and Moses; an allusion here and a quotation there would have been quite sufficient for his purpose to make his Jewish Christian congregation feel at home. It would of course have been much easier if there had been ten Beatitudes to correspond to the original Ten Commandments and indeed energetic efforts have been

made to cause the numbers to correspond. Scholarly
arithmetic has contrived as few as six and as many as ten
Beatitudes, depending on how the passage is read. For the
purposes of exposition I am assuming that there are nine –
a crude computation based on nothing more significant
than the number of times which the word 'blessed' occurs.
It so happens that the passage from Ecclesiasticus
previously quoted also specifies nine sources of blessedness. If there is one thing certain from evidence elsewhere
in Matthew's Gospel it is that he was familiar with the
book Ecclesiasticus and was deeply, even if sometimes
unconsciously, influenced by it. If Matthew had access to
any Beatitudes-style sayings and wished to use them as a
framework for the whole Sermon then he had a model
ready to hand in Ecclesiasticus which would have been as
familiar to his hearers as it was to him.

The 'imaginary scribe' struggling with the intellectual
and spiritual consequences of the separation between the
synagogue and the Church would have felt that his
innermost problems were at least understood if not
entirely resolved. He was still engaged in the age-long
pursuit of his people of 'blessedness', even though the
pursuit was to be conducted by different means with a
somewhat different end, even though his ultimate
authority was no longer Moses but Jesus. No Jewish
Christian need feel that he was being disloyal to Moses or
that he was now adrift on wholly uncharted seas without
the Law to guide him. I stand amazed at the skill and
subtlety of the author of this Gospel who so exactly
perceived the needs of the congregation to which this
Gospel was addressed. But the success of his enterprise
depended upon the extent to which he himself was aware
of the ancient traditions of his people reflected in Law and
poetry, in psalms and prophecy. The Beatitudes are
almost meaningless to a modern reader unless he is
prepared to make the effort of imagination which is
required to see himself as a member of that congregation,

defenceless and puzzled, as he viewed the breach widening between the faith which had once sustained him and his ancestors and the faith which he had lately embraced, who wondered at the contrast between the 'new teaching' and the well-tried formulas of the past, who had to get used to the fact that new wine could no longer be contained in the old bottles. This was the situation of many a believer in those early days of the Church; we have to understand his problems. if we are to appreciate Matthew's tentative solution to them. We have to feel for our 'imaginary scribe' in his torment of mind and spirit – and we may even find it helpful in our understanding of the Church today, torn as it is between claims of tradition and the crying need for innovation.

The fact that the one term 'the Beatitudes' has been given to this series of sayings in Matthew 5 obscures the fact that despite their common formula they are various in character. In some of them blessedness is seen in an attitude of mind – the poor in spirit, the meek, the merciful, the pure in heart. In others blessedness is attached to particular circumstances which can hardly be contrived or sought. Thus, those who have been given cause to mourn are blessed and those who are persecuted. It is the word 'blessed' which gives the Beatitudes in the New Testament and the Old such unity as they enjoy. It is to the meaning of this word 'blessed' that we now turn, to avoid unnecessary repetition when we come to the expositions later in this book.

Every human soul nurtures within itself some desire, some aspiration, some hope, the achievement of which in his view constitutes the supreme happiness – and it varies from century to century and from nation to nation. At times it has been death in battle; for some it has meant intellectual achievement. To some it means absence of pain, or sexual fulfilment. To some it means little more than an amorphous state of well-being induced by drink or drugs or fierce ascetic exercises. For 'My Fair Lady' it was 'lots of chocolates for me to eat'. Such aspirations and hopes have little in common with each other except that they exist and colour the mental scenery of us all in one way or another. It is not surprising therefore that the Hebrew people were so preoccupied with 'blessedness'; it represented for them their particular brand of hope or aspiration expressed in a striking variety of ways in the Psalms and the Wisdom literature. Of course, the Hebrews enjoyed the crude delights common to all nations – victory in battle, prosperity on the farm, a large family, a peaceful old age, but underneath there ran a current of hope which transcended mere good fortune.

So there was a blessedness in not walking in the council of the wicked (Psalm 1: 1), there was blessedness in trusting God (Psalm 2: 12), in having sins forgiven (Psalm 32: 1), in caring for the poor (Psalm 41: 1), in frequenting the temple (Psalm 84: 4), in being chastened by God (Psalm 94: 12) and above all, so the Psalmists of the later period of Jewish history proclaimed, in walking in the Law of the Lord and keeping his testimonies (Psalm 119: 1, 2). So our imaginary scribe when he heard the Beatitudes read in the early Christian congregations of the Near East would have found them familiar – but in other respects revolutionary. He could hardly have conceived the idea that the highest good was to be found in poverty, or grief, or persecution. These were inescapable evils to be borne with patience but hardly to be enjoyed. But perhaps if he had been thoroughly familiar with the Book of Job he might be able to make room in his mind for such a thought. For was it not true that it was in his extremes of pain and isolation that Job found the ultimate blessedness in a transcendent experience of God?

Then Job replied to the Lord:
'I know that you can do all things; no plan of yours can be thwarted. You asked, "Who is this that obscures my counsel without knowledge?" Surely I spoke of things I did not understand, things too wonderful for me to know. You said,

"Listen now, and I will speak, I will question you, and you
shall answer me." My ears had heard of you but now my eyes
have seen you. Therefore I despise myself and repent in dust
and ashes.' (Job 42: 1-6).

And so Job in mourning for his family and in the midst of
dire illness found the happiness which he had not found
when his table was frequented by his children, when his
barns were full and his future seemingly secure. But it has
to be said that it is a form of blessedness which not many of
us would seek for ourselves.

The time has now come to study the meaning of the
word 'blessed', bearing in mind what we have already seen
– that we must allow for variations in meaning imposed by
the process of transmission through which the word
'blessed' has passed. On the lips of the psalmist it was a
Hebrew word, on the Mount of the Beatitudes it was an
Aramaic word. To the author of Matthew's Gospel it was a
Greek word. We had better start with the Greek word,
which is the language which lies immediately behind our
English translations. The word is *Makarios*. Some
translators, notably J. B. Phillips, rendered the word 'how
happy are . . .' and that is reasonable because the classical
Greek usage of the word does mean happy and is normally
applied to the happy state of the gods above earthly
sufferings and labours.[5] Even in this early usage, however,
happiness is not conceived simply in terms of high spirits
or physical health or a happy marriage; it is somehow
characteristic of the gods. But the use of the word *Makarios*
in Matthew's mind would have been controlled by its use
in the Septuagint, a Greek translation of the Hebrew Bible
dating from the third century B.C. and widely used by both
Jews and Christians as a substitute for the Hebrew text.
But the authors of the Septuagint would themselves have
been controlled by the Hebrew text in front of them.
*Makarios* is a Greek rendering of the Hebrew word *esher*.
The word *esher* in a variety of forms is used over fifty times
in the Old Testament and was associated in the Hebrew

mind with fullness of life, earthly blessings, wife and
children, beauty, riches, honour and wisdom. But it 'was
saved from degenerating into a mere equivalence with
pagan notions of happiness by the fact that these outward
blessings were regarded as tokens of the divine favour, the
rewards bestowed upon righteousness, and so were
associated with the feelings of religious gratitude and
trust.'[6] It is interesting in this regard to observe that the
word commonly used in Greek for good fortune or
happiness is never used in the Septuagint or in the New
Testament and this better than any other observation
characterises the difference between 'blessedness' in the
Hebrew-Christian sense and 'blessedness' in the pagan
sense. I can hardly do better than quote again from the
admirable article in the *Encyclopaedia of Religion and
Ethics* from which I have quoted above:

> In its fundamental nature Christian blessedness appears as an
> inward spiritual experience. In setting forth his doctrine
> regarding it, Jesus vindicated the high idealism of those poet-
> saints of the Old Testament who had risen to a point of
> understanding the blessedness of the man who makes Jahweh
> his trust, while at the same time he repudiated the prevailing
> popular conceptions as in the blessings of the Messianic
> kingdom. In Matthew the list of The Beatitudes begins and
> ends with a declaration of the blessedness that lies in
> possessing the kingdom of Heaven ... it is in those experiences
> of ethereal trust and love and fellowship which result from
> knowing God through Jesus Christ as our God and father, that
> the essence of Christian blessedness lies.

Perhaps I may be permitted another quotation to illustrate
the same point taken from a modern *Dictionary of
Christian Spirituality*:[7]

> In recording The Beatitudes by which Jesus pronounced his
> disciples blessed the Evangelists use a Greek word *Makarios*,
> which means not ordinary happiness but rather the happiness

of the gods. What Jesus is promising his followers then is not
the happiness of fulfilled pleasure but the bliss of communion
with God.

It is this which makes Christian blessedness so striking an
experience and the Beatitudes so revolutionary a way of
looking at life. Our 'imaginary scribe' on the basis of his
own knowledge of the Scriptures would not have been
unprepared for this revelation, but nevertheless he would
have found the Beatitudes revolutionary and deeply
disturbing. As the author of this book, I sympathise with
him; they make our normal hopes and aspirations which
fill our waking hours and even perhaps our sleeping hours
extremely tawdry; they challenge our habitual desires for
comfort, luxury and success; they can demolish a life
laboriously built on worldly expectations; they can make a
man's past look like a waste of time; they summon him to
an uncomfortable pilgrimage on earth sustained only by
the hope of the eternal and the true. They do not make
good bedtime reading. They do not make a suitable
accompaniment for the school prize-giving or for
retirement speeches at the end of a long and successful
career in business – or for that matter in the Church. They
make the foundations of the house we have built tremble.
They are more alarming than the thunders and lightnings
of Sinai. They brook no contradiction.

We have so far spoken about the Beatitudes as if we
know what they are. But what are they? It is perhaps easier
to say what they are not. They are not items of legislation.
What Dr. Sandmel said about the Sermon on the Mount is
even more true about the Beatitudes – 'they are simul-
taneously unreservedly lofty and as legislation unreservedly impractical.'[8] No legislation, conservative or
socialist, could be built on the principle that the poor are
blessed or that the persecuted inherit the kingdom of God.
But they do not comprise an ethical system either, if we
understand ethical in the normal sense as 'connected with
moral action, connected with duties, moral feelings,

morality'. For there is nothing moral about being persecuted or about having lost your father in a car crash. The poor are not necessarily conspicuously moral in their attitudes to others and the merciful cannot rely on receiving mercy in this world. There is little in history or personal experience to support the belief that the meek will inherit the earth. Nor do they comprise what you might call a manifesto for Church life. Christians are not more conspicuously successful than their worldly counterparts in exhibiting the attitudes described in the Beatitudes. I am far myself from being poor in spirit, or meek, or merciful or pure in heart. I have not been conspicuously successful as a peacemaker and I have not had an opportunity of testing my reaction to persecution.

Even for the 'interim period' which Schweitzer proposed as his explanation of the Sermon on the Mount, the Beatitudes were not much in evidence in the life of the Christian Church. They are not counsels of perfection designed just for our mortification in failing to fulfil them. Perhaps we get nearer to the truth when we see them as the fruits of experience. The Scriptures abound with illustrations of the way in which the poor proved to be rich, in which loss proved to be gain, in which the pure in heart did see God and the merciful had mercy shown to them. Some of those who were persecuted did indeed receive a kingdom, those who were evil-spoken of in their day were later honoured as prophets and martyrs. There could hardly be any more striking comment on the way of life suggested by the Beatitudes than this passage from St. Paul in 2 Corinthians 4, as that great Apostle reflects on his experience of life in one of the earliest documents of the New Testament:

But we have this treasure in jars of clay to show that this all-surpassing power is from God and not from us. We are hard pressed on every side, but not crushed; perplexed, but not in despair; persecuted, but not abandoned; struck down, but not destroyed. We always carry around in our body the death of

Jesus, so that the life of Jesus may also be revealed in our body. For we who are alive are always being given over to death for Jesus' sake, so that his life may be revealed in our mortal body. So then, death is at work in us, but life is at work in you.

It is written, 'I believed; therefore I have spoken'. With that same spirit of faith we also believe and therefore speak, because we know that the one who raised the Lord Jesus from the dead will also raise us with Jesus and present us with you in his presence. All this is for your benefit, so that the grace that is reaching more and more people may cause thanksgiving to overflow to the glory of God. Therefore we do not lose heart. Though outwardly we are wasting away, yet inwardly we are being renewed day by day. For our light and momentary troubles are achieving for us an eternal glory that far outweighs them all. So we fix our eyes not on what is seen, but on what is unseen. For what is seen is temporary, but what is unseen is eternal.

The Beatitudes are not in the imperative form as the Ten Commandments were, but in the indicative form; they are descriptive of the blessedness which lights upon a man not as a result of moral effort or a brave stoicism, but as a consequence of faith in the living God. So it was for the saints of old; so it is for the saints today; so it will be for the saints to come. Blessedness is not the reward for good works, it is the concomitant of humble faith in the God who gives us liberally all good things to enjoy.

*Part Two*

# THE BEATITUDES

## Chapter 5

# BLESSED ARE THE POOR IN SPIRIT, FOR THEIRS IS THE KINGDOM OF HEAVEN

It is not obvious to the poor that the poor are blessed; it is not obvious to the rich either. My visits to London occasionally take me under the arch of Charing Cross Bridge. It is not obvious to me that those elderly men and women who huddle together in fair weather and foul under that bridge, lying on a newspaper mattress and clothed at best in the discarded garments of the wealthy, are blessed. It did not occur to me, braving the streets of Calcutta in the Second World War, that the beggars depending on the patrimony of six square feet of pavement and utterly dependent on the passer-by for sustenance, were blessed. In visiting as I did occasionally an old men's hostel in Liverpool I did not find these words welling up in my mind – 'blessed are the poor'. As Hans Kung rightly says,[1] 'poverty may teach men to pray but it also teaches them to curse. Poverty, suffering, hunger are misery not bliss.'

To make these obvious points is just to expose the problem raised by the Beatitude either in St. Luke – 'blessed are you poor' or in St. Matthew – 'blessed are the poor in spirit'. I have already taken time to draw your attention to the general background of the Sermon on the Mount, of Jesus who gave the Sermon, and of Matthew who recorded it, but now we have to be more specific and ask what is the background of this first Beatitude in particular?

What did the words mean in the mind of Jesus and in the minds of those who first heard them? We are already acquainted with the language problem: how we are to understand a sermon delivered in Aramaic and subsequently translated into Greek which is a non-Semitic language, resting upon a non-Semitic culture and attuned to non-Semitic habits of thought. So we have to look first at the Greek word, then at the Hebrew word which it normally translates, and then at the usage of the word in first-century Galilee. The Greek word behind our word 'poor' means what we expect it to mean. It means 'destitute', to lead the life of a beggar. It denotes the complete destitution which forces the poor to seek the help of others by begging,[2] and it is certainly used in this way in the New Testament and especially in St. Luke's Gospel, where the word is more frequent than anywhere else in the New Testament. So, 'when you give a banquet, invite the poor, the crippled, the lame, the blind' (Luke 14: 13). One of the parables peculiar to Luke makes the straight distinction between 'a rich man who was dressed in purple and fine linen and lived in luxury every day' and a certain beggar (poor) named Lazarus who was laid at his gate full of sores and desiring to be fed with the crumbs that fell from the rich man's table (Luke 16: 19–21). Zacchaeus promised to distribute his ill-gotten gains to the poor (Luke 19: 8). And it was a certain poor widow who was praised by Our Lord who 'out of her poverty put in all that she had to live on' (Luke 21: 1–4, R.V.). Luke rightly represents this as an inescapable element in the activity and the teaching of Jesus which we cannot evade.

No amount of discussion can conceal the fact that Jesus was a partisan for the poor, the mourning, the hungry, the failures, the powerless, the insignificant. The rich who heap up for themselves treasures which rust and moths consume and which thieves can steal, who give their heart to wealth, he presents in all their miserliness as a shocking example. Success, social advancement mean nothing to him: anyone who exalts himself will be humbled and vice versa. He has no interest in the people who are secure and sheltered, attached to the transitory goods of this world.[3]

Bishop David Sheppard was right to entitle his book *God's Bias to the Poor*. Blessed are the poor if only because thereby they are delivered from the perils of the rich. Matthew, Mark and Luke all record that most radical of sayings – 'It is easier for a camel to go through the eye of a needle than for a rich man to enter the kingdom of God' (Mark 10: 25 and parallels). But if this were all that could be said then I and indeed most of my readers have no hope of eternal life. We are all relatively rich. We all live in 'palaces' in comparison with the poor of Kerala in South India. We all enjoy labour-saving appliances which are not available to the greater part of mankind. We have cars and summer holidays and, even in Socialist states, second homes. We draw on the resources of the whole world for our menus. We consume more in a day than a peasant farmer in Bangladesh consumes in a month. We throw away what would be untold abundance to a beggar in the Third World. Like Dives in his wealthy home, we are clothed in purple and fine linen and fare sumptuously every day, often unaware of and inattentive to the poor man at our gate, much less the poor man on the other side of the world. If Luke's account is to be believed the day will come when we shall be in torment, and Lazarus will be in Abraham's bosom – with a great impassable gulf between us for ever.

I do not seek to escape from the dread decisions which such teaching seems to require of all of us, but I do have to make you aware of other aspects of poverty which not even the poor can ignore and which may indeed be even more unwelcome to the rich. The Greek word which we translate 'poor' is common in the Septuagint (the Greek

version of the Old Testament). In the great majority of
cases it stands as a translation of one Hebrew word and it is
this Hebrew word which constitutes the background
which I promised to uncover before you. It covers a wide
range of meaning far beyond the Greek word which
translates it. It means to be bowed down, afflicted, to be
depressed, downcast, to be poor, needy, to be humble or
oppressed.[4] Just to show the diversity of meaning of which
the word is capable I make the point that it is the word
translated 'meek' and applied to Moses (Numbers 12: 3).
The word exhibits a certain development of meaning from
earlier usage in the Old Testament to its later usage, but
'from the very outset the term carries with it a
complementary religious and ethical content in so far as
the poor are considered in their divinely willed fullness of
life.'[5] This is amply illustrated in the Psalms where the
word 'poor' does not exclusively refer to the destitute or the
mendicant. You can be poor and needy (Psalm 70: 5) but
you can also be 'poor and sorrowful' (Psalm 69: 29). You
can be poor and of a contrite spirit (Isaiah 66: 2) That is
why Dr. Manson was able to say:

> In the Judaism of the last two centuries B.C. the term was
> practically a synonym for 'saintly or pious'. The use of the
> word poor in this way goes back to the days of the Seleucid rule
> in Palestine. Then it was the poor above all who remained
> faithful to their religion and the Law. The well-to-do upper
> classes in Jerusalem allowed themselves to be tainted with
> heathenism. Hence 'rich' tends to mean worldly and
> irreligious and 'poor' the opposite. In Matthew the paraphrase
> 'poor in spirit' is an attempt to make this fact clear.[6]

'In Matthew the paraphrase "poor in spirit"' – Dr.
Manson thus raises the issue of the two versions of the first
Beatitude. St. Luke records that Our Lord said 'blessed are
you poor', Matthew records that Jesus said 'blessed are the
poor in spirit'. We have to go back to the mountain of
Beatitudes therefore and ask – what did Our Lord actually

say and what did He mean? As you will expect by now, there is no easy answer to this question. In fact, there is no generally accepted answer at all. Radicals in the social field would naturally say that the original form of the saying was as recorded in Luke – a blunt assertion elsewhere to be found in St. Luke's Gospel that the poor were on the way to eternal life and the rich on the way to hell. St. Luke himself and indeed the sources of his Gospel before him may have believed just that. It may account for the emphasis in his Gospel on the poor. It may explain why in his record of Jesus' first sermon in the synagogue at Nazareth he actually said that he had been anointed to preach good news to the poor (Luke 4: 18). But Luke was a Gentile, a convert to the Jewish faith perhaps, but as is obvious not only from the Gospel but from the Acts of the Apostles, not always acquainted with the inwardness of the faith which he had embraced. To him, a Greek speaker, 'poor' meant poor and that was that, much as it would mean to us when we hear the English read in church. But Matthew was a Jew, possibly even a Rabbi, and he never ceases to struggle in his Gospel to convey to his readers the subtleties of which he himself is aware.

It is an accepted principle of textual scholarship that it is the 'hard reading' which is always to be preferred if there are variants in the text itself or apparent disagreements between the writers of the Synoptic Gospels. On the surface, therefore, the Lucan form of the Beatitudes has to be more convincing simply because it would present seemingly intolerable challenges to the early Church which included rich and poor, privileged and under-privileged, aristocrats and proletariat, scholars and journeymen. Would St. Paul, for example, have made as many converts as he did if he had insisted that only the poor or those who made themselves poor could enter the kingdom? Would this not have excluded the well-educated Greek or the learned Rabbi from participation in the life of the Church, and thus have deprived the Church of what was absolutely essential for its survival, intellectual power and social acceptability?

It is unlikely that Matthew had Luke's Gospel in front of him when he wrote, but he may have had the same source material and it would be possible to argue with Matthew that his version of the Beatitude was softening it, dulling the edge of the sword which divided rich from poor, heaven from hell, Dives from Lazarus. On the other hand, Matthew would undoubtedly have been aware of the original meaning of the Hebrew word and he would have been well versed in its contemporary usage. There is a sense in which he was heightening the challenge of the Beatitude if, as Dr. Manson suggests, he supplied the words 'in spirit', because that leaves us rich and poor alike, Dives and Lazarus in the same position before the judgment seat of God. The poor man may be far from being poor in spirit. The rich man may occasionally exhibit just that attribute in his dealings with God and with his neighbours. Indeed, Jesus Himself was not poor in the normally accepted sense. The story of the birth of Jesus in an outhouse in Bethlehem is in terms of this discussion quite beyond the point. Symbolic though it may be, the circumstances were created by the exigencies of travel rather than by lack of money. He did not belong to the proletariat; He inherited a business from His father. He was self-employed. He became a 'mendicant' only in the sense that He sacrificed the securities of home and employment for the life of a wandering evangelist dependent upon the resources of others.

Matthew's 'paraphrase' is, therefore, intended to deliver us from the crude distinction between rich and poor. 'This Beatitude is poles removed from the caricatures of it which appear in political and social manifestos.'[7] There is another consideration which bears upon Matthew's version of the Beatitude. For the greater part of the first century A.D. Christians constituted in the minds of the public yet another Jewish sect. They had not proceeded very far along the road to what Dr. Sanders calls 'self-definition',[8] and the outsider would have been hard-pressed to distinguish between some of them. For example, there were the Essenes of whom, despite painstaking research, little is known –but what little is known makes it certain that they laid great store by voluntary poverty. Goods were held in common; they chose to live in singularly inhospitable places and they practised the most extreme asceticism. The other example would not have been available to us if this book had been written forty years ago. But in 1947 an Arab boy wandering on the shores of the Dead Sea stumbled upon a cache in one of the caves which abound there. The contents of this cache have absorbed the attention of scholars ever since. Subsequent excavation has uncovered a building oc-cupied from approximately 125 B.C. until A.D. 68 when its occupants apparently fled before the threat of the Roman armies, and before fleeing hid their precious documents in the surrounding caves. This is what Dr. Gaster has to say about the characteristics of the sect to which we are introduced by the Dead Sea Scrolls:

We are introduced by the Dead Sea Scrolls to a group of people who believed that they constituted the true and ideal congregation of Israel, a small remnant that had stayed faithful to the traditional covenant and that was thereby ensuring the continuance of God's people and the eventual cleansing of His land from the stain of guilt. The members of the community conceived of themselves as repeating in a later age the experience of their remote forefathers in the days of Moses. When they left the cities and villages and repaired to the desert, they pictured themselves as going out into the wilderness to receive a new covenant.[9]

The discovery of the Dead Sea Scrolls would not have aroused the interest it did had not some of the earlier commentators on the Scrolls publicised their view on the striking resemblance between the Qumran community and the early stages of the Christian Church. The Qumran sect and the Christian Church both believed themselves to represent the new Israel following the apostasy of the old Israel. Both of them emphasised the role of a 'teacher of righteousness'. Both of them looked forward to the end of the age and the collapse of the present world order. And – and this is our immediate point – both of them exalted poverty, and the Qumran community was even known as 'the community of the poor'.

In the light of more recent research the resemblances are perhaps less striking than the contrasts. In his latest essay on the subject Dr. Vermes says:

> One significant conclusion emerges from these consider-ations. If the Scrolls exerted any influence on the New Testament – and it is reasonable to assume that they did – they will have done so not on Jesus himself, to whom the bulk of Qumran doctrine will have been alien if not repugnant, but on Paul, John and other leaders of the new Church. Their use, that is to say, would reside in throwing light on the Christianity of the Apostolic age and in showing more clearly than ever before negatively what Jesus was not, rather than that He was.[10]

'What Jesus was not'. This would presumably have been as apparent to the author of Matthew's Gospel as it is to Dr. Vermes, and he would therefore have been at pains to distance the Church to which he belonged and for which he wrote from other sects which superficially seemed to resemble it. It is not difficult to see therefore why he insisted on the version – 'blessed are the poor in spirit' rather than the Lucan version – 'blessed are you poor'.

This excursus on the linguistic and social background of the Beatitude will have proved its worth if it helps to deliver us from preconceived notions about what the Beatitude means. Its meaning is controlled in Matthew's mind by the history of its use not only in the Old Testament but in contemporary Judaism, of which Dr.

Manson has said 'in the Judaism of the last two centuries B.C. the term "poor" was practically a synonym for Hasid, i.e. saintly or pious.'[11] To put it another way, the Beatitude is more concerned with our relationship with God than it is with our place in society. If you turn back to Dr. Goulder's diagram illustrating the unity of the Sermon on the Mount, you will see that in his view the whole Sermon is derived from or summarised by the Beatitudes. You will have to take account of the fact that he asserts, and I am unable to dispute it, that 'it was an ancient Jewish practice if a series of matters were to be expounded, to set them out in order and then give the exposition in reverse.'[12] Thus the preacher of today is apt to say 'This is my text – and I am going to expound it in three sections, *a*, *b* and *c*,' and does so. His Rabbinic counterpart, however, would have said 'This is my text (e.g. "blessed are the poor in spirit"). I am going to expound it under sections *a*, *b* and *c*' – and then begins at *c* and works his way back to *a*. This may seem a very perverse way of proceeding, but if Dr. Goulder is to be believed this is how it was.

The part of the Sermon therefore which illustrates the first Beatitude is towards the end of the Sermon (Matthew 7: 7–11):

Ask and it will be given to you; seek and you will find; knock and the door will be opened to you. For everyone who asks receives; he who seeks finds; and to him who knocks, the door will be opened. Which of you, if his son asks for bread, will give him a stone? Or if he asks for a fish, will give him a snake? If you, then, though you are evil, know how to give good gifts to your children, how much more will your Father in heaven give good gifts to those who ask him!

Dr. Goulder in fact provides his own paraphrase of the Beatitude – 'blessed are the beggars with respect to God, destitute before heaven the men of prayer.'[13] 'It is beggars who ask, seek, knock; they hammer on the gates of heaven and are not refused.' This interpretation does not depend on the argument about the exact structure of the Sermon on the Mount because illustrations abound in the Old Testament which are at least capable of the same interpretation. May I by way of illustration take an out-of-the-way, little-known passage from the book of Genesis:

> But Sarah saw that the son whom Hagar the Egyptian had borne to Abraham was mocking, and she said to Abraham, 'Get rid of that slave woman and her son, for that slave woman's son will never share in the inheritance with my son Isaac.'
>
> The matter distressed Abraham greatly because it concerned his son. But God said to him, 'Do not be so distressed about the boy and your maidservant. Listen to whatever Sarah tells you, because it is through Isaac that your offspring will be reckoned. I will make the son of the maidservant into a nation also, because he is your offspring.'
>
> Early the next morning Abraham took some food and a skin of water and gave them to Hagar. He set them on her shoulders and then sent her off with the boy. She went on her way and wandered in the desert of Beersheba. When the water in the skin was gone, she put the boy under one of the bushes. Then she went off and sat down nearby, about a bow-shot away, for she thought, 'I cannot watch the boy die'. And as she sat there nearby, she began to sob.
>
> God heard the boy crying, and the angel of God called to Hagar from heaven and said to her, 'What is the matter, Hagar? Do not be afraid; God has heard the boy crying as he lies there. Lift the boy up and take him by the hand, for I will make him into a great nation.'
>
> Then God opened her eyes and she saw a well of water. So she went and filled the skin with water and gave the boy a drink.
>
> God was with the boy as he grew up. He lived in the desert and became an archer. While he was living in the Desert of Paran, his mother got a wife for him from Egypt. (Genesis 21: 9–21).

Sarah had conceived a son in her old age and resented the presence of the son whom Abraham's maidservant, Hagar, had borne to him. There is nothing endearing about the attitude of Sarah or heroic about Abraham's conduct. Abraham did what he was told and got rid of his unfortunate maidservant. He offended against every rule in the social worker's book – unfair dismissal, racial discrimination, unspeakable cruelty to mother and child. But this story is of course not meant to be a study of appropriate social attitudes; it is intended to reveal a relationship between Hagar and the God of Israel which exactly epitomises the attitude of the poor in spirit. Hagar had no legal claim on Abraham. She had a child totally dependent on her. She was utterly without resources. She was alone in the desert. No wonder she lifted up her voice and wept – there was nothing else to do. But in this ultimate extremity she cried to the only God she knew, the God of Abraham, she hammered on the gate of heaven and she was not refused. In that sense the 'poor in spirit' are blessed. A well of water opens up before them. In their extremity they find the only ultimate satisfaction there is to be found on earth.

It is not just money that blocks the way:

> We have great possessions not in the least because we are very rich in terms of money, for indeed most people are not, but because we have great possessions in the way of pre-conceived ideas, confidence in our own judgment and the ideas with which we happen to be familiar, spiritual pride born of academic distinction, sentimental or material attachment to institutions and organisations, habits of life that we have no desire to renounce, concern for human respect or perhaps fear of public ridicule, or a vested interest in worldly honour and distinction.[14]

When faced with the first Beatitude in this sense few of us can escape the judgment. Emmet Fox goes on to say:

> Why was not the Christ message received with acclaim by the ecclesiastics of Jerusalem? Because they had great possessions,

possessions of Rabbinical learning, possessions of public honour and importance, authoritative offices as the official teachers of religion, and these possessions they would have had to sacrifice in order to accept the spiritual teaching. The humble and the unlearned folk who heard the master gladly were happy in having no such possessions to tempt them away from the truth.

I feel the weight of that utterance as one who has enjoyed at least some of the privileges accorded to the 'ecclesiastics of Jerusalem', as an official teacher of religion and an archbishop to boot. But I am no longer at the centre of things; I am undistracted by ecclesiastical schemes and objectives; so I am exposed once more to the inescapable challenge of the Gospel: 'you say, "I am rich; I have acquired wealth and do not need a thing." But you do not realise that you are wretched, pitiful, poor, blind and naked' (Revelation 3: 17). Like the Laodiceans, I have always been 'wretched and miserable, and poor and blind and naked', but it is fairly easy to allow 'possessions' of whatever form to convince you that you are rich and have need of nothing. There are obstacles to blessedness much more dangerous and deep-rooted than a comfortable house and an encouraging bank balance. It is possible to be a deeply religious man and yet to miss the point. We do not know whether Nicodemus was a rich man, but we do know that he was a 'master in Israel', a member of the Sanhedrin, a scholar of weight and reputation. The conversation with Jesus was his 'midnight hour' when all men must unmask. In that moment he knew that he was poor and blind and naked, and at that same moment heaven opened its gates to him. He discovered a blessedness that he never knew in the days of his spiritual affluence. In that sense if not in that sense alone he was 'born again'.

## Chapter 6

# BLESSED ARE THEY THAT MOURN FOR THEY WILL BE COMFORTED

As if there are not complications enough already, I have now to acquaint the reader with another complication, and that is that some ancient manuscripts reverse the order of the second and third Beatitudes. The argument for and against is well summarised by Dr. Farrer.[1] However, I do not myself think that the arguments for this reversal are so overwhelmingly powerful that we must accept them. So now in line with the more familiar order we turn to 'blessed are they that mourn'.

On the surface this seems a most unlikely proposition. I remember a child's funeral when I was a parish priest – the tiny, white hardboard coffin, the slow walk to the far end of the churchyard, the two parents distracted with grief and, as I afterwards discovered, grief combined with a certain sense of guilt; the few friends supporting them, bewildered by what they took to be a wholly arbitrary, inexplicable event without reason or hope.

Or, if you are old enough to do so, recall the Second World War and the telegram arriving just before lunch to inform the newly married wife or the anxious mother that he was 'missing believed killed'. Or, nearer our own day, the Aberfan disaster when one wet morning the slag heap above the village school burst and engulfed teachers and children in unforgettable disaster. Even the death of a pet dog can produce well-nigh unbearable grief in the mind of a child – or for that matter in the mind of an adult, as I know for myself full well. Where, in such instances of mourning, is blessedness to be found? Furthermore, whereas it is possible that we shall never endure abject poverty in this life, it is scarcely possible that we can altogether avoid the experience of grief. It is an inescapable factor in human life and it casts its shadow long before. All our lives we are subject to bondage through the fear of death (Hebrews 2: 15) whether it be our own death or somebody else's. But Our Lord would have been as vividly aware as we are of the threat of death. The lily fades, the sparrow falls to the ground, buildings collapse on people, men perish in war and are subject to fatal, irreversible illness. Jesus lived in a world where children were not protected either from the facts of life or from the facts of death, and He lived amongst a racial group where long and excruciating rituals accompanied death. Jesus experienced grief Himself in the death of a much-loved friend, Lazarus, and the Garden of Gethsemane bears witness to the dread which had accompanied the thought of His own coming death. So He was not unfamiliar with grief when He said that those who mourned were blessed. We have to ask therefore – what did He mean, or to put it more obliquely, what did Matthew think that He meant when he recorded these words?

As was the case with the definition of the word 'poor' so with the word 'mourn'. In English it also invariably means an emotion created by the death of a relative or friend. In the Hebrew word which lies behind the Greek word it certainly meant that, but a great deal more.

The Laws of mourning were very minute. The general time of mourning was seven days during which the mourner was forbidden to work, wash, anoint himself, or wear his shoes. For seven days the mourner might not read in the Law, the Prophets or the Talmud because it was a 'joy' to do so. The mourner was allowed during this period to read only the

Books of Job, Jeremiah, Lamentation and the 'Laws of Mourning'. He had to sit away from his dead with his head tied up and on the first day he might not wear his phylacteries. He was forbidden to shave his head or his neck or do anything which might be considered to be for his comfort. He could take no part in rejoicings and the rent in his garments was to be seen for thirty days. Even a poor man and one who lived on charity was forbidden to work for these days but after that time he might do work secretly for his maintenance or his wife might spin in his house. Travelling with goods was forbidden and no business even at the risk of loss could be transacted by himself or his families or his servants. The mourner was allowed to eat only in his own house. He might eat no flesh and drink no wine, nor could he ask blessing before or after food. He might not leave town for thirty days and in the case of mourning for a parent he might not go out of town for the first year until his friends told him to do so. After the death of a wife a widower might not marry for a year but if his wife had died childless or if she had left young children he might marry after seven days. A mourner being 'free' must attend the synagogue; when he appeared the congregation faced him as he entered and said 'blessed is he that comforteth the mourner.'[2]

It was blessed to comfort the mourner but the ritual scarcely suggests that it was blessed to mourn. I recall what it felt like when I was staying in a kibbutz in Israel when news came in of casualties and deaths on the front – the whole community was tense with pain. Given the fact that Jesus was familiar with the rituals surrounding death in His day, presumably He must have mourned the death of Joseph at some point in His early life. What therefore did He mean?

It is possible for the expositor to discharge his obligations by transferring the blessedness attached to mourning entirely to the future. And this is, in fact, what St. Luke seems to do – 'Woe to you who laugh now, for you will mourn and weep' (Luke 6: 25). So in Luke's mind the Beatitude represents just a reversal of fortune, in much the same way as Lazarus enjoyed and Dives suffered a reversal

of fortune in the life to come. But I doubt whether that was
Matthew's intention despite the powerful advocacy of Dr.
Bultmann[3] 'the blessing of the mourners in Matthew 5: 4 is
to be taken eschatologically. It takes up the prophetic
promises.' There is more to be said to mourners who sit on
a dark day in a cold church or in a warm crematorium
chapel than 'you will be comforted in heaven'. So unless
we take Dr. Bultmann's view, we are left questioning.

It may be helpful if we do the simple thing and consult a
Hebrew concordance on the range of meanings attached to
the Hebrew word 'to mourn'. Samuel, it is said, mourned
for Saul long before Saul was dead (1 Samuel 15: 35).
Isaiah could speak of the gates of Jerusalem mourning and
the earth mourning and the new wine mourning. The
people of Israel mourned for the dereliction and poverty of
Jerusalem (Joel 1: 9). Ezra mourned because of the trespass
of the people (Ezra 10: 6). So, although the word is
frequently used to describe mourning for the dead, it is not
used exclusively in that sense. This view is supported by
Dr. Goulder[4] - 'it is the humble penitent mourning for his
sins in ashes and sackcloth who is promised the comfort of
God, not the merely unhappy or deprived.' The language
of mourning is in fact very frequent indeed in the writings
of the Hebrews, even apart from the frequent incidence of
the word to mourn. There is a whole category of psalms
which are variously called lamentations or dirges, of
which Psalm 22 is one of the most famous examples, given
that the opening verse was, according to the evangelists,
uttered by Jesus Himself in the last extremities of pain and
suffering:

My God, my God, why have you forsaken me?
Why are you so far from saving me,
so far from the words of my groaning?
O my God, I cry out by day, but you do not answer,
by night, and am not silent...
I am poured out like water,
and all my bones are out of joint,

My heart has turned to wax;
It has melted away within me.
My strength is dried up like a potsherd,
and my tongue sticks to the roof of my mouth;
you lay me in the dust of death.
Dogs have surrounded me;
a band of evil men has encircled me,
they have pierced my hands and my feet.
I can count all my bones;
people stare and gloat over me.
They divide my garments among them
and cast lots for my clothing.
But you, O Lord, be not far off;
O my Strength, come quickly to help me. (Psalm 22: 1-2,
14-19)

If indeed the opening words of this Psalm were on Our
Lord's lips, it is evidence of grief and bewilderment in His
own life within which he yet found comfort as the
psalmist did:

For He has not despised or disdained
the suffering of the afflicted one;
He has not hidden his face from him
but has listened to his cry for help.
From you comes the theme of my praise in the great assembly;
before those who fear you will I fulfil my vows.
The poor will eat and be satisfied;
they who seek the Lord will praise him –
may your hearts live for ever!
All the ends of the earth
will remember and turn to the Lord,
and all the families of the nations
will bow down before him,
for dominion belongs to the Lord
and he rules over the nations. (Psalm 22: 24-28)

But in addition to the psalter there is a book actually called
'Lamentations', a series of dirges, ostensibly by an eye
witness of the fall of Jerusalem in 586 B.C., in which the

author mourns the destruction of Jerusalem, and the unspeakable fate of those who had lived in it. The prophets too are rich in the language of mourning where the word 'to mourn' is used over twenty times. But perhaps at the same time we could note too that they are rich in the language of comfort, for example:

> The Spirit of the Sovereign Lord is on me,
> because the Lord has anointed me
> to preach good news to the poor.
> He has sent me to bind up the brokenhearted,
> to proclaim freedom for the captives
> and release from darkness for the prisoners,
> to proclaim the year of the Lord's favour
> and the day of vengeance of our God,
> to comfort all who mourn,
> and provide for those who grieve in Zion –
> to bestow on them a crown of beauty
> instead of ashes,
> the oil of gladness
> instead of mourning,
> and a garment of praise
> instead of a spirit of despair.
> They will be called oaks of righteousness,
> a planting of the Lord
> for the display of his splendour. (Isaiah 61: 1-3)

It will not have escaped you that this passage was quoted by Our Lord Himself in His first sermon at Nazareth. Even at that early stage in His ministry He was preparing to comfort those that mourned, to bestow on them the oil of joy in place of mourning, to clothe those who believed in Him with a garment of praise in place of the spirit of heaviness.

But we must not be confined pedantically to the vocabulary of mourning in the Old Testament. The passages I have quoted serve only to illustrate the fact that the word 'to mourn' connoted far more to the Hebrew mind than it does normally to ours. There is a very wide range of experience reflected in the Old Testament which could be described as 'mourning'. But mourning for what? I offer one or two obvious examples which if they do no more, signify an experience much wider and deeper than the experience of personal bereavement. First, there is the experience of adversity. The Book of Job opens with a hair-raising description of the adversities which fell upon this good man, but we are told 'In all this, Job did not sin by charging God with wrongdoing.' (Job 1: 22)

The author of the book is not out to make our blood curdle with an unrivalled succession of disasters. He is addressing himself to the universal problem of mankind and unlike some contemporary thinkers actually proposing an explanation for it. The great poem which is the centrepiece of the book depends for its force upon the prologue and the epilogue. The whole point of the story was that Job was a good man and a pious believer (although not a Hebrew). His adversities were therefore, in the religious climate of the poet's day, inexplicable. Job himself refused to believe that his sufferings were due, as his comforters suggested, to previous wrongdoings. But he also believed in the power and providence of God and refused to curse Him. Somewhere between these two facile explanations lies the truth. The truth in the author's mind was that there is indeed blessedness to be had in 'mourning'. That is the only acceptable explanation of the dread facts of human existence which otherwise defy explanation. In the poet's view, the adversities of Job had led to a transforming experience of God which had never been available to him in the days of his prosperity. The Book of Job could indeed have been composed round the text 'blessed are they that mourn'.

Let me now take a quite different example, the Book Ecclesiastes. In this case it is not adversity which is the problem, but unfailing prosperity;

I, the Teacher, was king over Israel in Jerusalem. I devoted myself to study and to explore by wisdom all that is done under heaven. What a heavy burden God has laid on men! I have seen all the things that are done under the sun; all of them are meaningless, a chasing after the wind.

What is twisted cannot be straightened;
what is lacking cannot be counted.

I thought to myself, 'Look, I have grown and increased in wisdom more than anyone who has ruled over Jerusalem before me; I have experienced much of wisdom and knowledge.' Then I applied myself to the understanding of wisdom, and also of madness and folly, but I learned that this, too, is a chasing after the wind.

For with much wisdom comes much sorrow;
the more knowledge, the more grief. (Ecclesiastes 1: 12–18)

This wise man, whoever he was, had everything in his favour. He had no anxieties about where the next meal was coming from. He was not engaged in heavy, unrewarding toil; he was well favoured, rich and learned; he enjoyed the prestige which the Hebrews accorded to the 'wise man'. But he could find no comfort in a world which seemed from his point of view full of comfort.

Yet when I surveyed all that my hands had done
and what I had toiled to achieve,
everything was meaningless, a chasing after the wind;
nothing was gained under the sun. (Ecclesiastes 2: 11)

His problem was that he enjoyed everything that the world could offer and found in it only vanity. This is in some ways a much more painful experience than the man who can account for his unhappiness in terms of adversity. It probably explains why the suicide rate is highest in affluent, well-developed countries. It explains why technological progress seems to coincide with a desperate need for tranquillisers and a terrifying addiction to drugs. The day labourer who lays himself down at night can at least console himself with thoughts of leisure and comfort

and imagine that all would be well if he were in a position
to enjoy them. But not so Ecclesiastes. The book ends with
one of the most beautiful, and at the same time the most
haunting, passages anywhere to be found in Holy
Scripture:

> Remember your Creator
> in the days of your youth,
> before the days of trouble come
> and the years approach when you will say,
> 'I find no pleasure in them' –
> before the sun and the light
> and the moon and the stars grow dark,
> and the clouds return after the rain;
> when the keepers of the house tremble,
> and the strong men stoop,
> when the grinders cease because they are few,
> and those looking through the windows grow dim;
> when the doors to the street are closed
> and the sound of grinding fades;
> when men rise up at the sound of birds,
> but all their songs grow faint;
> when men are afraid of heights
> and of dangers in the streets;
> when the almond tree blossoms
> and the grasshopper drags himself along
> and desire no longer is stirred.
> Then man goes to his eternal home
> and mourners go about the streets.
> Remember him – before the silver cord is severed,
> or the golden bowl is broken;
> before the pitcher is shattered at the spring,
> or the wheel broken at the well,
> and the dust returns to the ground it came from,
> and the spirit returns to God who gave it.
> 'Meaningless! Meaningless!' says the Teacher,
> 'Everything is meaningless!' (Ecclesiastes 12: 1–6)

This is a man who went mourning all his days, not out of
bereavement or out of adversity, but out of a comfortable

enjoyment of the good things of life which in the alchemy of his own mind turned to dust. It is the testimony of a man who observes his fellow passengers on board the cruise liner, dancing, making love, eating fine dinners, flirting with other men's wives, gathering rosebuds while they may, and observes them with the painful sense that this is a doom-laden ship and its passengers are on the way to extinction with nothing to show for all their labours or their pleasures. Such a man, as Bonhoeffer puts it[5]

> sees that for all the jollity on board the ship is beginning to sink. The world dreams of progress, of power and of the future, but the disciples meditate on the end, the Last Judgment and the coming of the Kingdom. So while the world keeps holiday he stands aside and while the world sings 'gather ye rosebuds while you may' he mourns.

Hilaire Belloc felt the same way:

> Though unbelieving as a beast she didn't worry in the least
> But drank as hard as she was able
> And sang and danced upon the table.

But the Hebrew experience embraced more than bereavement, adversity or prosperity. It embraced, in a way peculiar to the Hebrew people, mourning for sin. Samuel mourned for Saul's sin long before he mourned his death. The prophets mourned the iniquities of Jerusalem long before they mourned its demise. David mourned his own sin with Bathsheba at least as much as he mourned the death of Jonathan or the death of Absalom, his son. Jeremiah mourned the unthinking dependence of Israel's rulers upon worldly aids more than he mourned the death struggles of a damned city. This sense of mourning for personal and national sins is no better exemplified than in the famous passage from Isaiah 53:

> He grew up before him like a tender shoot,

and like a root out of dry ground.
He had no beauty or majesty to attract us to him,
nothing in his appearance that we should desire him.
He was despised and rejected by men,
a man of sorrows, and familiar with suffering.
Like one from whom men hide their faces
he was despised, and we esteemed him not.
Surely he took up our infirmities
and carried our sorrows,
yet we considered him stricken by God,
smitten by him, and afflicted.
But he was pierced for our transgressions,
he was crushed for our iniquities;
the punishment that brought us peace was upon him,
and by his wounds we are healed.
We all, like sheep, have gone astray,
each of us has turned to his own way;
and the Lord has laid on him
the iniquity of us all.
He was oppressed and afflicted,
yet he did not open his mouth;
he was led like a lamb to the slaughter,
and as a sheep before her shearers is silent,
so he did not open his mouth.
By oppression and judgment he was taken away.
And who can speak of his descendants?
For he was cut off from the land of the living;
for the transgression of my people he was stricken.
He was assigned a grave with the wicked,
and with the rich in his death,
though he had done no violence,
nor was any deceit in his mouth.
Yet it was the Lord's will to crush him and cause him to suffer,
and though the Lord makes his life a guilt offering,
he will see his offspring and prolong his days,
and the will of the Lord will prosper in his hand.
After the suffering of his soul,
he will see the light of life and be satisfied;
by his knowledge my righteous servant will justify many,
and he will bear their iniquities. (Isaiah 53: 2-11)

It is no accident that the Christian Church from its very earliest days has associated this chapter with the sufferings of Christ. Our Lord too went mourning all his days; mourning the spiritual death of those ruthless men who sat in Moses' seat in Jerusalem, long before their physical death at the hands of the Romans forty years later; mourning the volatile and insubstantial dreams of those violent enthusiasts for freedom in Galilee, long before they paid the penalty for their revolt; mourning the obtuseness and blindness of his own disciples as he struggled to convey to them the Word of life. Luther translates the word 'mourn' with the phrase 'sorrow-bearing' and that translation perhaps enlarges our understanding of what the primitive Church felt when they associated Christ with the suffering servant – 'surely he has borne our griefs and carried our sorrows.'

Dr. Leonard Hodgson was Regius professor in Oxford when I was a student there immediately after the Second World War. In common with many other ex-servicemen we sat regularly at his feet admiring his learning and cogency and well aware of the concessions he was making to men whose knowledge of theology, such as it was, had been acquired in barrack rooms and prison camps. At the base of his own exposition of Christian doctrine lay a principle which he repeated over and over again for succeeding generations of students. It went something like this – 'if men of that day and of that environment, believing what they did about the world, expressed themselves in this way, how ought we today to express those same truths in our particular environment believing what we believe about the world?' This has been a valuable guide to me ever since, and ought always to be in mind when we attempt to apply the lessons of the past to the present. We have built up a picture of an intellectual and spiritual environment surrounding this Beatitude – rather laboriously you may think, but there is no short cut to understanding the world in which Christ lived, so different from ours in almost every aspect of human life. The language was different, the intellectual climate was different, the social milieu was different, and for all those differences we have to make allowances before we can offer any persuasive view to our own world of those mysterious words – 'blessed are those who mourn'.

Yes, everything was different except the fundamental human condition to which these words were first addressed. We remain mortal, and perish like the grass in the fields; we lose our loved ones as surely as Martha and Mary lost Lazarus or the widow of Nain lost her son; we have to suffer grievous anxiety about the sickness of a beloved child just as Jairus suffered on behalf of his daughter and the father at the foot of the Mount of Transfiguration suffered about his son. Even when we are free from personal anxieties of this kind we are shadowed by the thought of social anarchy and the disintegration of world order; we fear the bomb in much the same way as the Ancient World feared some indescribable disaster at the end of time and watched anxiously for its coming. In all these respects we are no different from our forefathers of two thousand years ago who actually heard the Sermon on the Mount, or heard it read and commented on in the congregations of Syria or the little conventicles of Greece. There would have been mourners amongst them mourning the death of parent or child the previous week, mourners bowed down with adversity of one kind or another, mourners wealthy enough to enjoy the good things of life but sick at heart, mourners who looked back over the past with grief for the things they had done or had failed to do, for the sins they had committed or had wanted to commit, mourners lamenting a disastrous relationship with husband or wife or parent or child. And they would hear, these mourners, not just that there was a good time coming beyond the sky where everything would be put right, but that in the midst of their sorrows blessedness was possible.

If that was what they believed then, what can we believe now? This is the most important question that anyone can ever ask. We are all bounded with mortality and the evidences of it are all around us in other people's lives if not in our own. Can it be true that the savage conditions of life on earth may be the very conditions under which we may experience blessing? Can the mourners smile, can the anxious rise up, can the sick rejoice, can the fearful laugh and sing? It is not a matter of 'dancing on the table', it is a matter of perceiving the truth about our condition and rejoicing in it. I say that this is the most important question we ever have to ask, but of course I speak only for myself. Like Job, I have known adversities, although in comparison with his very minor ones, in which I have been dimly conscious of a certain quietness and joy within, like the man who hears a familiar stream flowing on in the midst of a thunderstorm. But I have also been conscious even from childhood of the sense of vanity and emptiness which characterised Ecclesiastes' view of life – no sudden pain, no drastic deprivation, no consuming sorrow, but a dull awareness of the transitoriness of life and of the vanity of human desires. It falls short of clinical depression but it darkens the sun and imparts a certain sadness to even the most beautiful surroundings. 'The daughters of music shall be brought low ... man goeth to his long home and the mourners go about the streets' (Ecclesiastes 12: 4-5). Of all the human conditions that is the one most likely to threaten faith and to exclude joy, to extinguish hope and create despair. But there is something salvific about it. That is how life is and no amount of 'dancing on the table' can conceal the fact. That is how life is, but God created it, as Ecclesiastes continued to believe, and if God created it, and if God is good, then it must have some purpose. The author of the Book of Job was 'a infinitely more confident man than the author of the book of Ecclesiastes and he roundly asserted that it was the mourner, if he does not curse God in his mourning, who discovers the truth behind all appearances, who discovers personal reality at the heart of all things. The moment will steal upon him silently when God will be no longer the subject of learned debate or a mere syllable on the breath of man, but the loving creator who is high and lifted up, yet who is at the same time near to him who is of a contrite and humble spirit. That is blessedness indeed and our 'slight afflictions' as St. Paul calls them are as nothing in the balance, yielding as they do an eternal weight of glory (2 Corinthians 4: 17). They are but for a moment; glory is for ever.

As so often it is the Psalms which anticipate some of the profoundest utterances of Our Lord and this Beatitude is no exception. I quote now from Psalm 84: 1-6:

How lovely is your dwelling place,
O Lord Almighty!
My soul yearns, even faints
for the courts of the Lord;
my heart and my flesh cry out
for the living God.
Even the sparrow has found a home,
and the swallow a nest for herself,
where she may have her young –
a place near your altar,
O Lord Almighty, my King and my God.
Blessed are those who dwell in your house;
they are ever praising you.
Blessed are those whose strength is in you,
who have set their hearts on pilgrimage.
As they pass through the Valley of Baca,
they make it a place of springs;
the autumn rains also cover it with pools.

The last verse quoted above has been variously translated and I leave you with a few possibilities for your own contemplation when bowed down with adversity or bored with life or mourning the loss of a loved one or mourning for your sins.

Going through the vale of misery they use it for a well and the pools are filled with water. (Book of Common Prayer)

Passing through the valley of weeping they make it a place of springs. (R.V.)

When they pass through weary-glen, fountains flow for their refreshing. (Moffat)

As they pass through the dry valley of Baca it becomes a place of spring. (Good News Bible)

As they pass through the thirsty valley they find water from a spring and the Lord provides even men who lose their way with pools to quench their thirst. So they pass on from outer wall to inner and the God of Gods shows Himself in Zion. (New English Bible)

The words are different but they describe the same experience otherwise expressed in the more familiar words of Psalm 23:

Though I walk through the valley of the shadow of death, I will fear no evil: for Thou art with me; thy rod and thy staff they comfort me.

Yes indeed – blessed are those who mourn, for they shall be comforted, not only in the next world but in this.

*Chapter 7*

# BLESSED ARE THE MEEK FOR THEY WILL INHERIT THE EARTH

'Blessed are the meek for they will inherit the earth' – a paradoxical saying indeed which confronts the strong and the confident and the powerful of the earth. We might be prepared to believe that the meek will inherit the kingdom of heaven (for anything can happen there) but there is little evidence that they ever inherit the earth. Genghis Khan, Alexander of Macedon, Napoleon and Stalin may have had many qualities but meekness was not amongst them.

But the curious part about this saying of Jesus' is that it was not original to Him and was indeed a distinctive feature of Hebrew piety as it is portrayed in their Scriptures. The exact Greek words of the text occur in the Greek version of Psalm 37: 11 – 'the meek shall inherit the land and shall delight themselves in the abundance of peace'. The Hebrew word behind the Greek word is frequently used in the Psalms and elsewhere in the prophetic writings. The fact that the phrase in the Beatitudes corresponds so exactly with the phrase from the Psalms will perhaps create a question in the mind of the attentive reader, and that particular question has long been discussed in scholarly circles, both Jewish and Christian. The question is whether we can claim for Jesus of Nazareth the striking originality which is sometimes attributed to Him or whether we have to come to terms with the fact that much of Our Lord's teaching is to be found in the teaching of first-century Judaism. The argument is often, alas, conducted in a polemical vein by those on the one hand who wish to emphasise the supremacy of Christ, and on the other hand by those who wish to emphasise Jesus' debt to the religion of His forefathers. The argument is unlikely to be resolved when conducted in these terms, for we have seen in a previous chapter how seriously we have to take the fact that 'Jesus was a Jew' – brought up in a Jewish home, educated in a synagogue school, a member of the local synagogue and conditioned to believe that the sacred Scriptures of His people were indeed the word of God. His teaching abounds with quotations of or allusions to those same Scriptures. Even in the last extremities of pain and dereliction it is a sentence from the Psalms which is on His lips – 'My God, my God, why have you forsaken me?' (Mark 15: 34, Psalm 22: 1). The exact correspondence of the words of this Beatitude with the words of Psalm 37: 11 ought not therefore to surprise us. Jesus was not a guru, clutching lapidary utterances out of the air, but a Jewish teacher drawing freely upon the tradition from which His fellow teachers in Jewry also drew. In any case, the supposed contrast between originality and tradition scarcely obtains in any walk of life. The nature of history requires and progress demands that architects make houses from materials long used by previous architects, that musicians compose music with tonal values that others have identified, that poets use words which are meaningful only because they are familiar already to those who hear them. Painters either exhibit or revolt against earlier artistic traditions; they cannot ignore them.

This seeming diversion may be helpful in dealing with this particular Beatitude because its meaning almost more than any of the others depends upon the meaning of the word 'meek' already fixed in the tradition within which

Jesus thought and taught. That tradition was not entirely unaffected by the Hellenistic world in which Jesus and His companions lived. In that world meekness suggested a 'mild and gentle friendliness'; it is the opposite of roughness, bad temper, anger, contempt for others. The Hebrew word, however, is concerned much less with our attitudes to other men than with our attitudes to God. The meek man is 'one who feels that he is a servant in relation to God and who subjects himself to Him quietly and without resistance.'[1] Such an attitude towards God may issue in meekness towards men but it may not. In view of what we have supposed about Matthew's background, it is not surprising to find that the word appears often in the book Ecclesiasticus and because the book may not be in your version of the Bible I offer one or two examples from it:

The fear of the Lord is wisdom and instruction and in faith and meekness is His good pleasure. (1: 27, R.V.)
My son go on with thy business in meekness; so shalt thou be beloved of an acceptable man. (3: 17, R.V.)
Incline thine ear to a poor man, and answer him with peaceable words in meekness. (4: 8, R.V.)
My son, glorify thy soul in meekness and give it honour according to the worthiness thereof. (10: 28, R.V.)

But the most striking use of the word is to be found in Chapter 45 which reads as follows:

He brought out of him (Jacob) a man of mercy, which found favour in the sight of all flesh; a man beloved of God and men, even Moses, whose memorial is blessed. He made him like to the glory of the saints, and magnified him in the fears of his enemies. By his words he caused the wonders to cease; he glorified him in the sight of kings; he gave him commandment for his people, and shewed him part of his glory. He sanctified him in his faithfulness and meekness, he chose him out of all flesh. He made him to hear his voice, and led him into the thick darkness, and gave him commandments face to face, even the law of life and knowledge, that he might teach Jacob the covenant, and Israel his judgments. (Ecclesiasticus 45: 1-5, R.V.)

Moses' reputation for meekness enshrined in this passage did not derive from any so-called meekness or timidity before men. He stood before the Pharaoh unafraid, he led an intransigent people with force and subtlety through nearly forty years of pilgrimage. He was not afraid to exercise authority and he was a severe judge of his people's frailties and shortcomings. No 'meek' man this, as John Bunyan made clear in his story of Faithful's encounter with Moses:

> So soon as the man overtook me he was but a word and a blow for down he knocked me and laid me for dead. But when I was little come to myself again I asked him wherefor he served me so. He said because of my secret inclining to Adam the First and with that he struck me another deadly blow on the breast and beat me down backward as I lay at his feet as dead as before. So when I came to my self again I cried him mercy but he said I know not how to show mercy and with that he knocked me down again. He had doubtless made an end of me but that one came by and bid him forbear.

But this same Moses, so fierce and uncompromising in his relations with men, knew himself to be the servant of the most high God and conducted himself in God's presence 'quietly and without resistance'.

We have to allow, in assessing the meaning of this Beatitude, not only for the traditions of the fathers as represented in Scripture; we have to take account of movements and attitudes contemporary with Our Lord's life and ministry. There is no evidence that Our Lord was directly associated with the Dead Sea Sect but he could hardly have been wholly unaffected by it and by the verbal currency which it made familiar. The Qumran texts make much of meekness and as the texts may not be available to you I quote from Dr. Gaster's version of the *Manual of Discipline*:

> This is the way those spirits operate in the world for the enlightenment of man's heart, the making straight before him all the ways of righteousness and truth, the implanting in his heart of fear for the judgments of God. A spirit of humility, patience, abundant compassion, perpetual goodness, insight, discrimination, a sense of the divine power that is based at once upon an apprehension of God's works and a reliance on His plenteous mercy, a spirit of knowledge informing every plan of action, a zeal for righteous government, a hallowed mind in a controlled nature, abounding love for all who follow the truth, a self respecting purity which abhors all the taint of filth, a modesty of behaviour coupled with general prudence and an ability to hide within oneself the secrets of what one knows – these are the things that come to men in this world through communion with the spirit of truth. And the guerdon of all that walk in its ways is health and abundant well-being with long life and fruition of seed, along with eternal blessings and everlasting joy in the life everlasting, and the crown of glory and a robe of honour amid life perpetual.
>
> But to the spirit of perversity belong greed, remissness in right doing, wickedness and falsehood, pride and presumption, deception and guile, cruelty and abundant insolence, shortness of temper and a profusion of folly, arrogant passion...[2]

The word 'meekness' does not occur but observe the characteristic attitudes of the meek as they were represented in the community at Qumran – 'humility, patience, a sense of the divine power, a hallowed mind in a controlled nature' and all these set over against the characteristic attitudes of the world – 'pride and presumption, cruelty and abundant insolence, shortness of temper and profusion of folly.' It is noticeable too that the virtues prescribed by the Qumran sect are not exclusively associated with 'everlasting joy in the life everlasting' but with health and abundant well-being, with long life and fruition of seed. So, the third Beatitude would not have seemed to His hearers in the first half of the first century as outrageous or paradoxical as it may seem to us. The crowds who hung on his lips may well have included soldiers, busy businessmen out for a quick and profitable deal, ambitious men consumed with a desire for success, elderly ecclesiastics preoccupied with questions of status, young men looking for glory. They may have been far from meek themselves but they would know what was meant and they may even have had a lurking suspicion that in the end it would be the meek who inherited not only heaven but earth.

This is given particular point by the existence of another group within Israel which was actually represented, we are told, in the innermost group of Our Lord's disciples. The group included Simon the Zealot (Mark 3: 18). The Zealots were a group of fanatical Jews who opposed all forms of compromise with or accomodation to the imperial power. Their concern was to mount a successful rebellion against Rome, to throw off the yoke by whatever means were available to them. They were not all men of violence, but they certainly included a subgroup called the Sicarii, so named because of their habit of concealing long daggers under their clothes and their aptitude for knifing unwary Roman sentinels, or indeed sometimes fellow Jews who happened to disagree with them. Their attitude to Rome was much the same as the Stern gang's attitude to the British, nineteen hundred years later. If they had been in the crowds listening to Jesus they would have found the third Beatitude distinctly unpalatable – they were not meek before men, some of them were not meek before God either. They proposed to inherit the earth by other means. It is possible though by no means certain that Our Lord had such in mind when he said 'from the days of John the Baptist until now the kingdom of heaven suffereth violence, and men of violence take it by force' (Matthew: 11: 12, R.V.). The verse is irremediably obscure but the temper of it is certainly at variance with the temper of the Beatitude.[3] The point is made even more forcibly in the narrative of the arrest:

> The men stepped forward, seized Jesus and arrested him. With that, one of Jesus' companions reached for his sword, drew it out and struck the servant of the high priest, cutting off his ear.
>
> 'Put your sword back in its place,' Jesus said to him, 'for all who draw the sword will die by the sword. Do you think I cannot call on my Father, and he will at once put at my disposal more than twelve legions of angels? But how then would the Scriptures be fulfilled that say it must happen in this way?'
>
> At that time Jesus said to the crowd, 'Am I leading a rebellion, that you have come out with swords and clubs to capture me? Every day I sat in the temple courts teaching, and you did not arrest me. But this has all taken place that the writings of the prophets might be fulfilled.' Then all the disciples deserted him and fled. (Matthew 26: 50–56)

This is one more example of what Anthony Harvey describes as one of the 'constraints of history'. Jesus of Nazareth, like every other teacher, had to operate within the conventions of his day even although he was not inhibited by them. It is sometimes thought that it was the presence of a zealot amongst his innermost disciples which gave credibility to the charge that He was intent on revolution. He needed to reiterate the great truth already entrusted to His people in the Scriptures and elsewhere, that it was the meek who would inherit the earth, not the men of violence nor the political agitators or for that matter the Emperor in Rome or the High Priest in Jerusalem.

Perhaps I could end this linguistic and historical research into the meaning and use of the word 'meek' with this comprehensive and judicious quotation from the *Dictionary of Christ and the Gospels* (p. 160).[4] The author of the article is Dr. Adam Findlay:

Meekness is a virile and noble thing. The outward garb of meekness may indeed be worn by men to whom there are none of the robust and gracious qualities which make true meekness so worthy of admiration and honour. There are those who by natural disposition are timid and compliant who have not manliness enough to resent injustice, who do not retaliate when they are wronged simply because they dare not. Similarly, there are those who when slighted show no sign of resentment because they are too dull to feel an affront or because they are controlled by feelings of scorn or by consideration of self-interest and policy. Of none of these can it be said that he is meek nor does his conduct deserve our admiration. True meekness, which is worthy of all honour, is seen only in those who with an acute sense of wrong, control the natural impulse to show anger and to retaliate, not from fear or pride or policy or scorn of others, but because in obedience to the will of God they accept the provocation or wrong as discipline and as an opportunity for showing the divine spirit of patience and love. The meek man is not quick tempered or vindictive, because swayed by feelings of benevolence and love he remains master to himself. Where there is no love there is no meekness.

It is one thing to evaluate the meaning of the word 'meek' in the currency of Our Lord's day. It may be quite another to evaluate it in the currency of our own day and we have to ask now what are the implications of the Beatitude for the society in which we live, so different, so it would seem, from the society in which Our Lord lived. In Britain at least for the moment we are not a subject nation; such 'Messianic' aspirations as we have are not expressed by men with long daggers under their clothes; there are men of violence but no foreign power on which to vent their violence. Nevertheless, we live in a violent society and by that I do not mean just the violence of the streets or terraces or the subway; we live in a society where violence is expressed in a more sophisticated way which does not conflict with the law of the land. There are men who 'get things done' without regard to the effects on whose who

have things done to them. There are men intent on
preventing things being done regardless of the needs of the
general public. The touchstone of success is to achieve
power without necessarily reckoning with the obligations
or responsibilities of power. There is many a 'night of
long knives' in which the weapons of destruction are not
of the steel kind but are intrigue, innuendo, character
assassination, manipulation of votes, disparagement of
opponents; and the source of it all is a raging ambition
which often enough does not exactly prescribe its
objectives or provide any outline of the 'ideal society' to
which these men of violence are committed. So meekness
is by and large out of place; it is not seen as an engine of
progress, it is despised and seemingly powerless. It will
never inherit this land.

This land? The Greek word translated 'earth' in the
Beatitudes can also be translated 'land'. It was in this sense
that it was often used to describe the Promised Land. The
Beatitude in that form, therefore, would certainly arouse
in the minds of those who first heard it echoes of the land
which Israel itself had inherited. The disorderly mob who
came out of Egypt into that fierce and hostile wilderness
had at least one cause to be termed meek – they were
helpless, with the Egyptian forces behind them and the
desert ahead; they had no military resources, no provision
for the way, no knowledge of the route, no clear perception
of the land which lay at the end of it except that it was
inhabited by warlike people living largely within fortified
cities. They were not meek by intention, they had
meekness thrust upon them by the circumstances in which
they found themselves. Forty years later, hardened by the
wilderness into a formidable fighting force, they raged
through the land of Canaan burning down cities and
destroying their inhabitants, often perpetrating the
cruelties which accompanied war then, and still do. They
inherited the land but they were not meek.

The lessons appointed for Morning Prayer in the early

part of February are taken from the books of Maccabees written in about 100 B.C., describing the popular uprising by the Jews against their oppressors in a revolt which began in 167 B.C. The story unfolded is a story of the utmost heroism with tiny guerilla forces arrayed against the seemingly invincible power of the Seleucid empire. The following is a typical passage from 2 Maccabees 7:

> It came to pass also, that seven brethren with their mother were taken, and compelled by the king against the law to taste swine's flesh, and were tormented with scourges and whips. But one of them that spoke first said thus, What wouldest thou ask or learn of us? we are ready to die, rather than to transgress the laws of our fathers. Then the king, being in a rage, commanded pans and caldrons to be made hot; which forthwith being heated, he commanded to cut out the tongue of him that spake first, and to cut off the utmost parts of his body, the rest of his brethren and his mother looking on. Now when he was thus maimed in all his members, he commanded him being yet alive to be brought to the fire, and to be fried in the pan: and as the vapour of the pan was for a good space dispersed, they exhorted one another with the mother to die manfully, saying thus, The Lord God looketh upon us, and in truth hath comfort in us, as Moses in his song, which witnessed to their faces, declared, saying, And he shall be comforted in his servants. So when the first was dead after this manner, they brought the second to make him a mocking stock: and when they had pulled off the skin of his head with the hair, they asked him, Wilt thou eat, before thou be punished throughout every member of thy body? But he answered in his own language, and said, No. Wherefore he also received the next torment in order, as the former did. And when he was at the last gasp, he said, Thou like a fury takest us out of this present life, but the King of the world shall raise us up, who have died for his laws, unto everlasting life. After him was the third made a mocking stock: and when he was required, he put out his tongue, and that right soon, holding forth his hands manfully, and said courageously, These I had from heaven; and for his laws I despise them; and from him I hope to receive them again.

I will spare you the rest of the chapter because it is not agreeable reading even for us now so habituated to hideous violence of this kind. On the surface it would seem that the account of this heroic resistance by Israel is not dissimilar from the heroic exploits of Israel in their original conquest of the Promised Land. But there is a subtle, indefinable difference. The story of the Maccabees for all its ample references to divine assistance reads like the history of many a resistance movement in our own day – heroic, bloodthirsty and utterly ruthless in its pursuit of the given objective. The Maccabees were not meek and the land they 'inherited' did not long survive. Within two hundred years, torn by political rivalries and weakened by bitter defections within it, it fell victim to the Romans and ceased to be in any meaningful sense Israel's land.

Contrast to this story of the Maccabees, the story of Moses, Joshua and David. Over and over again the early leaders of Israel almost unwittingly exhibited something of the meekness which does inherit the land. 'They knew themselves to be servants in relation to God and subjected themselves to Him quietly and without resistance.' 'Fear ye not,' Moses said, 'stand still, and see the salvation of the Lord which He will work for you today. For the Egyptians whom ye have seen today, ye shall see them again no more for ever. The Lord shall fight for you, and ye shall hold your peace' (Exodus 14: 13–14, R.V.). And here is a passage from the Joshua narrative which exhibits the same kind of total reliance upon God:

Now when Joshua was near Jericho, he looked up and saw a man standing in front of him with a drawn sword in his hand. Joshua went up to him and asked, 'Are you for us or for our enemies?'

'Neither,' he replied, 'but as commander of the army of the Lord I have now come.' Then Joshua fell face down to the ground in reverence, and asked him, 'What message does my Lord have for his servant?' The commander of the Lord's army replied, 'Take off your sandals, for the place where you are standing is holy.' And Joshua did so. (Joshua 5: 13–15)

And here are words from one of the most famous narratives in the Bible, the story of the single combat between Goliath and David:

He looked David over and saw that he was only a boy, ruddy and handsome, and he despised him. He said to David, 'Am I a dog, that you come at me with sticks?' And the Philistine cursed David by his gods. 'Come here,' he said, 'and I'll give your flesh to the birds of the air and the beasts of the field!'
David said to the Philistine, 'You come against me with sword and spear and javelin, but I come against you in the name of the Lord Almighty, the God of the armies of Israel, whom you have defied. This day the Lord will hand you over to me, and I'll strike you down and cut off your head. Today I will give the carcasses of the Philistine army to the birds of the air and the beasts of the earth, and the whole world will know that there is a God in Israel. All those gathered here will know that it is not by sword or spear that the Lord saves, for the battle is the Lord's, and he will give all of you into our hands.'
As the Philistine moved closer to attack him, David ran quickly towards the battle line to meet him. Reaching into his bag and taking out a stone, he slung it and struck the Philistine on the forehead. The stone sank into his forehead, and he fell face down on the ground.
So David triumphed over the Philistine with a sling and a stone, without a sword in his hand he struck down the Philistine and killed him. (1 Samuel 17: 42–50)

These men were by no means meek in our commonly accepted use of the term, but they were meek in the sense in which the term is used in the third Beatitude. They knew their weakness; they had no hope of victory by their own sword; they were confronted by impossible odds and they looked in their meekness to the saving hand of God. Father Tugwell is right in saying that meekness is 'the moral spiritual attitude which is learned from helplessness.'[5]
The people of Israel 'inherited' the land; at least in their

best moments they knew that it had not been won by their skill or courage. To the more sensitive souls amongst the people this was a truth given greater credibility by the experiences through which Israel passed during their brief experience of nationhood – at risk from the powerful empires on their borders, often invaded, usually despised, a people of no account. So it is not surprising that Isaiah should speak approvingly of 'the man who is meek and of a contrite spirit and who trembles at the word of God' (Isaiah 66: 2) or that Zechariah should look forward to the day when the Messiah should come 'both meek and riding on an ass' (Zechariah 9: 9).

Matthew quotes a version of this passage in his account of the triumphal entry into Jerusalem. In his mind perhaps that action epitomised the life of Christ all the way through. Despite some children's hymns which suggest that He was, Jesus was not in the obvious sense of the term a meek man. He could be scathing about the attitudes of the rich and the powerful, he was an adroit and skilful debater in public, he cleansed the temple with a display of righteous anger, and there is a curious passage in Mark which suggests the dynamic power within, which only occasionally surfaces in public. It occurs in the early part of his ministry and is as follows:

A man with leprosy came to him and begged him on his knees, 'If you are willing, you can make me clean.'

Filled with compassion, Jesus reached out his hand and touched the man. 'I am willing,' he said. 'Be clean!' Immediately the leprosy left him and he was cured.

Jesus sent him away at once with a strong warning: 'See that you don't tell this to anyone. But go, show yourself to the priest and offer the sacrifices that Moses commanded for your cleansing, as a testimony to them.' Instead he went out and began to talk freely, spreading the news. As a result, Jesus could no longer enter a town openly but stayed outside in lonely places. Yet the people still came to him from everywhere. (Mark 1: 40–45)

The translation hardly does justice to the phrase in verse 43. The Greek word more commonly translated 'strictly charged' is very unusual and occurs elsewhere in the New Testament only at Matthew 9: 30 (the parallel passage), Mark 14: 5 and John 11: 33–38. It suggests a certain kind of fury only with great difficulty restrained. It is a powerful word, incompatible, we might suppose, with genuine meekness. Commentators differ as to why Jesus was so furious at his encounter with the leper. They will differ also about the significance of the word in the story of the raising of Lazarus:

> Jesus, once more deeply moved, came to the tomb. It was a cave with a stone laid across the entrance. 'Take away the stone,' he said. 'But, Lord,' said Martha, the sister of the dead man, 'by this time there is a bad odour, for he has been there four days.'
> Then Jesus said, 'Did I not tell you that if you believed, you would see the glory of God?'
> So they took away the stone. Then Jesus looked up and said, 'Father I thank you that you have heard me. I knew that you always hear me, but I said this for the benefit of the people standing here, that they may believe that you sent me.'
> When he had said this, Jesus called in a loud voice, 'Lazarus, come out!' The dead man came out, his hands and feet wrapped with strips of linen, and a cloth around his face.
> Jesus said to them, 'Take off the grave clothes and let him go.' (John 11: 38–44)

The translators have done their best but have scarcely done justice to the rare word that appears in the Greek version. Why was Our Lord so deeply moved? Why in such turmoil of spirit? Why apparently so 'furious' within?

I quote the story only to make the point that whatever the cause, the word suggests deep perturbation of spirit seemingly inconsistent with the genial and friendly bearing of 'the meek'. Nevertheless, in the sense in which the word 'meek' is used in the Psalms and Proverbs Jesus was a true son of Israel, a meek man, knowing his utter dependence on God in a world full of enemies. He did not propose his own destiny. He raised no standard, embraced no political cause, founded no party, sought nothing for himself and disowned the vengeful anger and impatience of his disciples. He could have summoned twelve legions of angels to his aid but refused to do so. He could have demolished Pilate's feeble arguments but kept silent. He could have come down from the Cross but chose to endure the pain and dereliction to the end. He achieved nothing, so it would seem, in His life, but in His death He conquered the world. He was the archetypal meek man who inherited the earth and those of us who believe in Him and follow Him in his meekness can inherit it too.

It would be unfair to leave the reader on this high note without showing some awareness of the acute dilemmas which meek men are subject to in a highly competitive society and in a world where totalitarian power seems to reign supreme. This is well illustrated by the life of Dietrich Bonhoeffer, a German pastor and teacher of outstanding academic ability who became involved in the abortive attempt to assassinate Hitler and to re-establish democratic government in Germany. Here was a man scholarly and sensitive, hardly equipped for exploits of derring-do, who never altogether came to terms with the role he felt himself called upon to play. In his own commentary on the Beatitude 'blessed are the meek'[6] he had said:

> The meek renounce every right of their own and live for the sake of Jesus Christ. When reproached they hold their peace, when treated with violence they endure it patiently, when men drive them from their presence they yield their ground. They will not go to Law to defend their rights or make a scene when they suffer injustice, nor do they insist on their legal rights. They are determined to leave their rights to God alone. They show by every word and gesture that they do not belong to this earth. Leave heaven to them says the world in its pity, that is

where they belong. But Jesus says 'they shall inherit the earth'. To those, the powerless and the disenfranchised, the very earth belongs. Those who now possess it by violence and injustice shall lose it and those who here have utterly renounced it, who are meek to the point of the cross, shall rule the new earth.

How was he, fervent and enthusiastic Christian as he was, to compromise as it would seem with the intrigue and violence by which Hitler was to be destroyed? Nevertheless, he came to feel that he was embarked on the right course to remove an evil thing from the earth and he used such means as were necessary to achieve that end. But he took this decision with open eyes, well aware of the possible political and spiritual consequences for himself. The project failed. He and his associates were arrested and imprisoned and one fine morning he was executed.

On the morning of the day some time between five and six o'clock the prisoners, among them Admiral Canaris, General Oster and Sack the Judge Advocate General, were led out of their cells and the verdicts read to them. Through the half-open door of a room in one of the huts I saw Pastor Bonhoeffer still in his prison clothes kneeling in fervent prayer to the Lord his God. The devotion and evident conviction of being heard that I saw in the prayer of this intensely captivating man moved me to the depths.

So the morning came. Now the prisoners were ordered to strip. They were led down a little flight of steps under the trees to the secluded place of execution. There was a pause – for the men about to die, time hung a moment suspended. Naked under the scaffold in the sweet spring woods Bonhoeffer knelt for the last time to pray. Five minutes later his life was ended.[7]

Brave beyond all expectations before his enemies, meek before God, Dietrich Bonhoeffer was an Israelite indeed. He died with the conviction still intact in his mind which he expressed at the end of his commentary on the Beatitude:

The renewal of the earth begins at Golgotha where the meek one died and from thence it will spread. When the Kingdom finally comes, the meek shall possess the earth.

## Chapter 8

# BLESSED ARE THEY THAT HUNGER AND THIRST AFTER RIGHTEOUSNESS FOR THEY WILL BE FILLED

The political activist, who may find it difficult to make any room in his philosophy for the poor in spirit or the mourners or the meek, can at least find in this Beatitude something to which he can respond. If there is a dominant theme for the twentieth century it is the pursuit of a more just and righteous society. Despite all the contradictions within it and the subsequent perversions of it, Marxism constitutes in the minds of those who adhere to it a positive hunger and thirst for a righteous society in which the gross inequalities of the capitalist system shall be removed, in which war will cease to be an instrument of policy, in which meaningless class distinctions will be abolished, in which slaves will be freed:

> The history of all hitherto existing society is a history of class struggles. Freeman and slave, patrician and plebeian, Lord and serf, Guildmaster and journeyman – in a word oppressor and oppressed stood in constant opposition to one another, carried on an uninterrupted now hidden, now open fight, a fight that each time ended either in a revolutionary reconstitution of society at large or in the common ruin of the contending classes... the modern bourgeois society that has sprouted from the ruins of feudal society has not done away

with class antagonisms, it has but established new classes, new conditions of oppression, new forms of struggle in place of the old ones... let the ruling classes tremble at a communist revolution, the proletarians have nothing to lose but their chains. They have a world to win. The working men of all countries unite. (Communist Manifesto)

Behind these stirring words and the violent expressions of the Communist Manifesto the figure of Karl Marx himself looms large and fearsome, a man consumed with anger at the present order of things and a burning desire to change them forever.

We know only too well the cost of this revolutionary zeal in the giant purges of the Stalinist regime, in the dead hand of an ever-growing bureaucracy, in the dominance of the State which Marx and his earliest followers trusted would wither away. But the man himself living in abject poverty for the greater part of his life, sacrificing home and family to his burning vision, bruised and wounded in the interminable feuds which disfigured early Communism, this man did hunger and thirst after righteousness. Surrounded as he was by all the evidences, as he took them to be, of a decaying and doomed society, he launched on the tide of revolutionary change. Perhaps we ought not to be surprised. Karl Marx was a Jew. His father had been officially received into the Church in 1817, a year before the birth of his eldest son, Karl:

The hostility of Karl Marx to everything connected with religion, and in particular with Judaism, may well be partly due to the peculiar and embarrassed situation in which such converts sometimes found themselves. Some escaped by becoming devout and even fanatical Christians, others by rebelling against all established religion. They suffered in proportion to their sensitiveness and intelligence. Both Heine and Disraeli were all their lives obsessed by the personal problem of their peculiar status; they neither renounced nor accepted it completely but mocked at or defended the religion of their fathers, or alternated between these attitudes, uneasily aware of their ambiguous position, perpetually suspicious of the latent contempt or condescension concealed beneath the fiction of their complete acceptance by the society in which they lived.[1]

But overt hostility to the religion of his fathers and indeed to all religion did not entirely erase his background from his mind. Could he have been wholly unfamiliar for example with the words of Amos:

'I hate, I despise your religious feasts;
I cannot stand your assemblies.
Even though you bring me burnt offerings and grain offerings,
I will not accept them.
Though you bring choice fellowship offerings,
I will have no regard for them.
Away with the noise of your songs!
I will not listen to the music of your harps.
But let justice roll on like a river,
righteousness like a never-failing stream!' (Amos 5: 21-24)

Marx was not the first nor the last to despise the solemn assembly, the burnt offerings and meal offerings, the noise of hymns and the melody of viols, and to envisage the day when judgment would roll down as waters and righteousness as a mighty stream.

So far we have been using the word 'righteousness' as if we knew what it meant. But if you have read the book this far you will know that the Beatitudes call for careful exegesis if we are to establish the meaning of 'poor' or 'mourn' or 'meek'. So, as with the other Beatitudes, we now have to ask what the word 'righteousness' meant in the context of Our Lord's life and ministry and in the political and religious climate of His day. Whatever it may have come to mean for us, we have to be assured that what it means for us is not inconsistent with what it meant for those eager listeners in Galilee in the first half of the first century.

Even a casual reader or hearer of the Scriptures will be aware that in the New Testament 'righteousness' is often associated with those who claimed to be the supreme practitioners of it, the Pharisees. For the sake of convenience I append various utterances in St. Matthew's Gospel which make or assume this association between Pharisees and righteousness:

While Jesus was having dinner at Matthew's house, many tax collectors and 'sinners' came and ate with him and his disciples. When the Pharisees saw this, they asked his disciples, 'Why does your teacher eat with tax collectors and "sinners"?' On hearing this, Jesus said, 'It is not the healthy who need a doctor, but the sick. But go and learn what this means: "I desire mercy, not sacrifice." For I have not come to call the righteous, but sinners.' (Matthew 9: 10-13)

'Do not think that I have come to abolish the Law or the Prophets; I have not come to abolish them but to fulfil them. I tell you the truth, until heaven and earth disappear, not the smallest letter, not the least stroke of a pen, will by any means disappear from the Law until everything is accomplished. Anyone who breaks one of the least of these commandments and teaches others to do the same will be called least in the kingdom of heaven, but whoever practises and teaches these commands will be called great in the kingdom of heaven. For I tell you that unless your righteousness surpasses that of the Pharisees and the teachers of the law, you will certainly not enter the kingdom of heaven.' (Matthew 5: 17-20)

'Woe to you, teachers of the law and Pharisees, you hypocrites! You are like whitewashed tombs, which look beautiful on the outside but on the inside are full of dead men's bones and everything unclean. In the same way, on the outside you appear to people as righteous but on the inside you are full of hypocrisy and wickedness.' (Matthew 23: 27-28)

But this association between the Pharisees and righteousness is not confined to St. Matthew's Gospel, prominent though it is in it. St. Luke suggests the same association in his parable of the Pharisee and the publican (Luke 18: 9–14).

So, we have to allow for the fact that Our Lord's teaching was given within a religious context where conflicting ideas of what constituted righteousness were current. The Pharisees have a bad press in the New Testament, undeservedly so in the minds of many scholars, but St. Matthew's Gospel, as we have seen, was written at a time when the Pharisaic party in Judaism was seriously at odds with the burgeoning Christian community. Pharisees and Christians were rivals for the allegiance of the Jewish people, and Matthew is likely to have emphasised rather than diminished the contrast between Pharisees and Christians in their understanding of righteousness. The argument is conducted with great force in the Epistle to the Romans where the word 'righteousness' is used thirty-eight times. Here is the classic passage in which the contrast between the two views of righteousness is expressed:

> But now a righteousness from God, apart from law, has been made known, to which the Law and the Prophets testify. This righteousness from God comes through faith in Jesus Christ to all who believe. There is no difference, for all have sinned and fall short of the glory of God. (Romans 3: 21–23)

The contrast is clear enough as one would expect in the writings of a man who was himself a Pharisee before he became a Christian. The Pharisees stood for strict obedience to the letter of the law as a means of achieving righteousness. The Christians stood for a faith in Christ as the way to righteousness – and the only way acceptable in God's sight. Amongst the Pharisees of Our Lord's day there were great and good men, deeply concerned for the future of Israel, devoted to the God of their fathers and heroic in their attempts to apply the Scriptures to everyday life. This much both they and Jesus of Nazareth had in common and this no doubt partly accounts for the sharpness of the disagreement between them. But it is not possible to evade the logic of Paul's argument – the Pharisees stood for righteousness of one kind, Jesus of Nazareth and Paul stood for righteousness of a different kind. We go to heaven with the scribes and Pharisees or we go to heaven with Jesus of Nazareth.[2] We might have wished that the argument could have been conducted with more charity on both sides but an argument there has to be. We need to know what sort of righteousness we are hungering and thirsting for if we are to be blessed in hungering and thirsting for it.

It is an unwilling tribute to the continuing influence of the New Testament that the word 'righteous' does not engage the sympathies of the average English reader – and that is largely because of the association made by the New Testament between righteousness and the Pharisees; it suggests the 'holier than thou' attitude, the critical spirit, rigidity of mind; it suggests a contrast between what a man professes and what he really thinks. The 'whited sepulchre' gleams disconcertingly before the eyes of the English reader when he hears the word 'righteousness'. A positive effort is therefore required to escape from these misleading images; it is necessary to go back behind the controversies of the first century to its antecedents in the Greek and Hebrew language.

The Greek word has a long history in classical literature. In that literature it largely described a man possessed of the cardinal virtues (prudence, justice, temperance, fortitude) and it was righteousness as so understood which would one day constitute the ideal society, the Utopia which provided the only escape there seemed to be for the Hellenistic man from the harsh and disagreeable realities of his political and social world. But when the Greek translators of the Old Testament used the word in the Septuagint they were controlled less by Greek models than by Hebrew models, as indeed was inevitable. The translation of any ancient document into a different language is bound to be misleading, but the Jewish exegetes were under obligation to approximate as nearly as possible to the meanings discerned in the Hebrew text in front of them. The Hebrew word does not deal in 'cardinal virtues' as if they were something which men could possess or acquire or achieve. For the Hebrews, righteousness implied relationships. Thus, 'a man is righteous when he meets certain claims which another has on him in virtue of relationship. Even the righteousness of God is primarily His covenantal role in fellowship with His people.'[3] We ought not to be surprised therefore that it was largely in this sense that the prophets summoned their people to righteousness and, if the frequency of the word in the Prophets is anything to go by, they summoned their people to righteousness with unremitting zeal. In the book of the prophet Isaiah alone the word righteousness is used fifty-one times. It is a long book but that frequency of usage is still an impressive witness to the importance of righteousness in the teaching of the Prophets. Like Amos, he perceived the close relationship between religion and conduct; like Amos, he decries religious enthusiasm if it blinds people's eyes to their true relationship with God and with other people:

> Hear the word of the Lord,
> you rulers of Sodom;
> listen to the law of our God,
> you people of Gomorrah!
> 'The multitude of your sacrifices –
> what are they to me?' says the Lord.
> 'I have more than enough of burnt offerings,
> of rams and the fat of fattened animals;
> I have no pleasure
> in the blood of bulls and lambs and goats,
> When you come to appear before me,
> who has asked this of you,
> this trampling of my courts?
> Stop bringing meaningless offerings!
> Your incense is detestable to me.

New Moons, Sabbaths and convocations –
I cannot bear your evil assemblies,
Your New Moon festivals and your appointed feasts,
my soul hates.
They have become a burden to me;
I am weary of hearing them.
When you spread out your hands in prayer,
I will hide my eyes from you;
even if you offer many prayers,
I will not listen.
Your hands are full of blood;
wash and make yourselves clean.
Take your evil deeds
out of my sight!
Stop doing wrong,
learn to do right!
Seek justice,
encourage the oppressed.
Defend the cause of the fatherless,
plead the case of the widow. (Isaiah 1: 10–17)

Righteousness, as he saw it, was not a matter of church attendance and festivals but of 'seeking judgment, relieving the oppressed, judging the fatherless, pleading for the widow.' The general epistle of St. James says much the same:

> Religion that God our father accepts as pure and faultless is this: to look after orphans and widows in their distress and to keep oneself from being polluted by the world. (James 1: 27)

I will not labour the point quoting extensively from the Prophets because this is a task which the reader or his study group can do for itself, by the simple expedient of consulting a concordance. But I draw your attention in particular to one passage which mirrors the coming ideal society as it was understood in the prophetic circles of Israel:

See, a king will reign in righteousness
and rulers will rule with justice.
Each man will be like a shelter from the wind
and a refuge from the storm,
like streams of water in the desert
and the shadow of a great rock in a thirsty land.
Then the eyes of those who see will no longer be closed,
and the ears of those who hear will listen.
The minds of the rash will know and understand,
and the stammering tongue will be fluent and clear.
No longer will the fool be called noble
nor the scoundrel be highly respected.
For the fool speaks folly,
his mind is busy with evil;
He practises ungodliness
and spreads error concerning the Lord;
the hungry he leaves empty
and from the thirsty he withholds water.
The scoundrel's methods are wicked,
he makes up evil schemes
to destroy the poor with lies,
even when the plea of the needy is just.
But the noble man makes noble plans,
and by noble deeds he stands. (Isaiah 32: 1-8)

I need hardly make the point that Karl Marx was in one
sense true to his ancestral tradition when he burned in
thought and word for a new earth and a new heaven
wherein dwelt righteousness. I hardly need to make the
other point too, that the society which Marx helped to
create bears little relation to this glowing picture born in
the mind of the great prophet Isaiah. Isaiah in common
with all the prophets perceived that the ideal society
would not be the product of political and economic forces
alone; it would be the product of health-giving relationships with God and with other men – a much more elusive
but a much more convincing manifesto.

The prophets thought their thoughts and uttered their
oracles in a religious community which was always at risk,

at risk from the imperial designs of the great powers surrounding it and at risk from the political and social solvents which threatened the community from within. It was always the temptation of the rulers (and they could well be forgiven for it), both out of fear and out of a genuine concern for the integrity of Israel, to seek advantage in the world by building armies, employing mercenary soldiers, acquiring economic power and making useful treaties. The prophets were consistently against such a policy, not because they were naive or unworldly, but because they perceived that the integrity of Israel woud be preserved only in so far as they fulfilled the purposes for which they had been called, and lived in accordance with God's will and God's law. Treaties in their view were a 'covenant with death' (Isaiah 28: 15). The important thing was to maintain a covenant with God. The city could only look for divine protection if it was a city of righteousness, a faithful city (Isaiah 1: 26-7). In the view of the later prophets it was the neglect of righteousness, not the neglect of the fortifications, which led to the ultimate humiliating collapse of Jerusalem and the deportation of its people. Early Zionism saw the return of Jews to the Promised Land in the nineteenth century not just as a political expedient but as an opportunity to build again a 'city of righteousness' in which God's will would be done and God's law observed in a programme of meticulous obedience.

The fall of Jerusalem in 586 B.C. created in the minds of those who survived either in Jerusalem or in exile a deep sense of guilt (as stunning defeat often does). Painful questions arose in the Jewish mind – why should this have happened to the chosen people of God? Why was the place God had chosen to put His name now a smoking ruin without temple or priesthood? The answer of the exilic prophets was consistent with the teaching of the pre-exilic prophets. They had foretold that a nation which departed from righteousness was a nation doomed to destruction.

That prophecy had now come true. When some of the exiles returned from Babylon during the reign of Cyrus they knew, unlike their predecessors in Jerusalem, that the future of Israel depended not on political alliances, armed force or economic prowess (all of which were far out of reach), but on building a righteous society which could earn or at least merit the approval of God and His divine protection.

It was not surprising therefore that the Law as it had developed over the centuries and was now codified became the resource to which the Jews looked for guidance and grace. If, so the argument ran, Ezra and Nehemiah could create a society in which the Law of God was meticulously observed, then they would be able to rely upon His protection and fulfil the purposes in the world for which they believed their people had been chosen. They would become the chosen people following the chosen way in the chosen land, forever secure and at peace. It was a magnificent ideal but it had within it the seeds of its own disintegration, and St. Paul, looking back over the centuries of his people's history, was quick to see it. This meticulous obedience to the letter of the Law engendered an attitude of mind which was indeed far from righteousness. It bred an attitude of mind in which Jewish groups competed with each other for merit, in which Jews sat in judgment upon other Jews, in which salvation was seen to be the product not of God's grace but of unremitting effort, in which all concerns for common humanity came to be submerged beneath the dominant concern for legal rectitude. The precise origin of the Pharisees is still a matter of dispute, but by the time of Our Lord they represented the ultimate term of a process which began with the return of Ezra to Jerusalem. They represented a form of Judaism with which St. Paul had identified, but which he later disclaimed. They represented a form of Judaism which perforce led to bitter conflict between Our Lord and the guardians of Israel and to ultimate

separation of the Christian community from its parent
body.

What had gone wrong? Ironically, in view of the heroic
efforts of the Jewish people to save themselves from
Hellenism, they had virtually succumbed to it. Righteousness was now seen as an achievement, a possession, a claim
to pre-eminence, an aspect of the ideal society, whereas
righteousness in its older usage concerned relationships –
relationships with God and with others which must take
precedence over any legal duties or rights, however fiercely
pursued. St. Paul was only harking back to an ancient
tradition when he insisted that 'Abraham believed God
and it was reckoned unto him for righteousness' (Romans
4: 3, R.V.) This is a quotation from Genesis 15: 6.
Whatever the date of Genesis (and that remains unknown
to us) the author of the book was an inheritor of the
ancient tradition which saw righteousness not as the
product of human effort, however heroic, but of a relationship with God. St. Paul was no innovator; he simply saw
with a clarity which eluded most of his contemporaries the
nature of the issue between Jews and Christians. I quote
now the whole passage in which this issue is pursued:

What then shall we say that Abraham, our forefather,
discovered in this matter? If, in fact, Abraham was justified by
works, he had something to boast about – but not before God.
What does the Scripture say? 'Abraham believed God, and it
was credited to him as righteousness.'

Now when a man works, his wages are not credited to him as
a gift, but as an obligation. However, to the man who does not
work but trusts God who justifies the wicked, his faith is
credited as righteousness. David says the same thing when he
speaks of the blessedness of the man to whom God credits
righteousness apart from works:

Blessed are they
whose trangressions are forgiven,
whose sins are covered.
Blessed is the man

whose sin the Lord will never count against him.'

Is this blessedness only for the circumcised, or also for the uncircumcised? We have been saying that Abraham's faith was credited to him as righteousness. Under what circumstances was it credited? Was it after he was circumcised, or before? It was not after, but before! And he received the sign of circumcising, a seal of the righteousness that he had by faith while he was still uncircumcised. So then, he is the father of all who believe but have not been circumcised, in order that righteousness might be credited to them. And he is also the father of the circumcised who not only are circumcised but who also walk in the footsteps of the faith that our father Abraham had before he was circumcised.

It was not through law that Abraham and his offspring received the promise that he would be heir of the world, but through the righteousness that comes by faith. For if those who live by law are heirs, faith has no value and the promise is worthless, because law brings wrath. And where there is no law there is no transgression.

Therefore, the promise comes by faith, so that it may be by grace and may be guaranteed to all Abraham's offspring – not only to those who are of the law but also to those who are of the faith of Abraham. He is the father of us all. As it is written, 'I have made you a father of many nations.' He is our father in the sight of God, in whom he believed – the God who gives life to the dead and calls things that are not as though they were.

Against all hope, Abraham in hope believed and so became the father of many nations, just as it had been said to him, 'So shall your offspring be.' Without weakening in his faith, he faced the fact that his body was as good as dead – since he was about a hundred years old – and that Sarah's womb was also dead. Yet he did not waver through unbelief regarding the promise of God, but was strengthened in his faith and gave glory to God, being fully persuaded that God had power to do what he had promised. This is why 'it was credited to him as righteousness.' The words 'it was credited to him' were written not for him alone, but also for us, to whom God will credit righteousness – for us who believe in him who raised Jesus our Lord from the dead. He was delivered over to death for our sins and was raised to life for our justification. (Romans 4)

It will come as no surprise to the reader that this particular chapter has been the source of bitter division not simply between Jews and Christians, but between competing groups within the Christian Church itself. Here is set forth in the starkest possible way the contrast between those who rely upon their own righteousness and those who rely for their righteousness upon God alone. It is only too easy to magnify the issue for polemical purposes but the issue remains, as Luther saw, crucial to the life of the Church. St. Paul and Luther and Wesley and many another had not only the New Testament on their side, but they had Abraham on their side too, and the prophets, and the wise men.

It must not be thought that this is an issue only for society as a whole or for the divine community; it rages within the heart of many an individual Jew or an individual Christian. The most obvious example within the sacred Scripture is the testimony of Job. The author of the book was amongst other things concerned with the nature of righteousness. 'I know that I am righteous' (Job 13: 18, R.V). 'My righteousness I hold fast and will not let it go, my heart shall not reproach me as long as I live' (Job 27: 6, R.V.). If any man, we might say, deserved divine protection it was Job; he had reached physical and spiritual heights seldom traversed or even attempted by other men. He was the wise man of the East, living at peace within himself and at peace with his neighbours. But his undoubted merits did not apparently earn the unqualified approval of Him who sits on the throne of the universe. He is subjected to every conceivable disaster, finds himself despised by the society in which he had been such a conspicuous ornament, and treated with contempt by the guardians of orthodoxy. What had gone wrong was that Job had come to rely upon himself for his own salvation. He was a pious man, a 'faithful churchman', but his own speeches in the Book betray the origins of his piety: if he kept the rules all would be well. But all was not well and it was only in the depths of his own pain and degradation that he discovered true righteousness, based upon a warm and living relationship with God which he had done nothing to create, and which was a sheer gift which he could either accept or refuse. He was a man who hungered and thirsted after righteousness and failed to find it, but was in the end fulfilled.

The same point is made in the story of the prodigal son, so relevant to our theme, in St. Luke's Gospel, Chapter 15. The parable is capable of unlimited application, but in its immediate context it is a comment on the difference between the righteousness of the Pharisees and the righteousness described by Jesus. The elder brother was meticulous in his duties on his father's farm and was devoted to his father's cause. He deserved well, so he thought, of his father's generosity. The younger brother deserved nothing. He had treated his father with contempt, he had pursued his own ends, he had enjoyed his brief pleasures, and now a beaten man he was on his way home. He rehearsed his speech beforehand but he never completed it. He was received with honour and love by the one whose love he had spurned. Righteousness does not depend on meticulous obedience but arises out of a sense of defeat or of shame and a new awareness of an old, indestructible relationship.

A man nearer our own time who in his own experience had proved this truth puts it this way:

The Jews place righteousness in keeping all the particulars of the law of Moses. Paul says faith in God was counted righteousness before Moses was born. You may answer Abraham was unjust in many things and by no means a righteous man. True, he was not a righteous man in any complete sense, his righteousness would never have satisfied Paul, neither you may be sure did it satisfy Abraham. But his faith was nevertheless righteousness and if it had not been counted to him for righteousness there would have been falsehood somewhere. Such faith as Abraham's is righteousness. It was no mere intellectual recognition of the existence of a God which is consistent with the deepest atheism, it was that faith which is one with action – 'he went out not knowing whither he went.' The very act of believing in God after such fashion that when the time of action comes the man will obey God, is the highest act, the deepest and loftiest righteousness of which man is capable and is at the root of all other righteousness.[4]

I turn back to the beginning of this chapter. Karl Marx was a Jew; he had a consuming desire for a new world in which righteousness would prevail. But it has not prevailed in societies which bear his name, and no amount of special pleading can hide that fact. I quote from the Epilogue of Kolakowski's great three-volume work, *The Main Currents of Marxism*. It is part of the epilogue but could well be read as an epitaph:

> Marx took over the romantic ideal of social unity, and communism realised it in the only way feasible in an industrial society, namely by a despotic system of government. The origin of this dream is to be found in the idealised image of the Greek city state. Marx seems to have imagined that once capitalists were done away with, the whole world could become a kind of Athenian agora. One had only to forbid private ownership of machines or land and, as if by magic, human beings would cease to be selfish and their interests would coincide in perfect harmony. Marxism affords no explanation of how this prophecy is founded or what reason there is to think that human interests will cease to conflict as soon as the means of production are nationalised.[5]

Christians cannot afford to feel superior. The kind of righteousness only too often after which we hunger and thirst is a righteousness more akin to late Judaism than to the teaching of the New Testament. Righteousness has become a thing of rules and causes and protests and heady ideals, a thing of political shreds and social patches. But we can at least disregard these shams and return to the rock from which we were hewn, learn again what it means to go out not knowing whither, to rejoice in that loving relationship with Him and with each other which is God's sheer gift to mankind through Christ. We shall always hunger and thirst for righteousness in society and for righteousness in ourselves, but we shall be hungering and thirsting for something that is real. The promise is that we shall be filled. I end with a quotation from a perceptive article by R.E.C. Brown in *A Dictionary of Christian Ethics* under the heading 'Righteousness'[6]:

> The Sermon on the Mount is no code of law which men can obey by an act of will. It describes the disposition a disciple is to develop and maintain. This development and maintenance is part of his creative activity which begins in God. This activity is not a matter of suppressing thoughts and wishes or forcing them to move in carefully chosen directions but of letting them follow in the wake of the attention given to events in the ceaseless divine-human creative activity. A legalist could say 'I have kept the law.' But creative righteousness has no like finality to offer; rather it has an air of uncompleted adventure such as known by explorers, inventors, artists and mystics. This freedom, this readiness to meet the new, make thinking and acting dangerous but creative righteousness is more concerned with truth and love than with safe behaviour.

## Chapter 9

# BLESSED ARE THE MERCIFUL FOR THEY WILL BE SHOWN MERCY

Translators of the Bible have an unenviable task and we must be merciful to them, not least with regard to this Beatitude. The word 'merciful' calls for a great deal of painstaking excavation. How painstaking may be deduced from a newly published concordance to the *Good News Bible*[1] which provides a thematic index, in which an attempt is made to suggest the many nuances of the word 'merciful'. Under 'mercy' see 'kind'; then follows a list of the various English words which occasionally do service for the Greek and Hebrew originals – 'compassion, concern, considerate, friendly, gentle, gracious, merciful, mercy, pity, spare, sympathy, tender'.

It would be instructive to compare that list with the news bulletin you saw on television last night or the newspaper you read this morning. There will I am afraid be few examples of the attributes of 'mercy'. We live in an age, not all that different from previous ones, which abounds with examples of cruelty to the young and lack of sympathy to the old, where ideologies are pursued in total and 'conscientious' disregard of the cost to those affected by them, where insensitive bureaucratic procedures obliterate mercy, where the pursuit of profit is narrowly conceived in commercial terms regardless of the price paid by individuals or minority groups. Rabid ideologues, fuelled more by hatred of mankind than by love of it, will cut off a finger here, an ear there, to convince the unhappy relatives that the hostage now in their hands is seriously at risk. Revolutionaries will proudly take credit for the latest bomb outrage and publicly glory in the number killed or maimed.

We are familiar enough with criminals robbing banks or holding up trains or assaulting security guards or terrorising hapless householders. What is perhaps new in our generation, or at least more prominent, is that atrocities are committed in the name of unexceptionable ideals and legitimate political ends. So it is that we live in a world defaced with cruelty masquerading as ideology, with terrorism pretending to be idealism, where the end is conceived to be so important that it justifies any means whatsoever. The first casualty of war, they say, is truth; the first casualty of social struggle, so it seems, is often mercy. But those of us who are associated with religion, be it Judaism, Hinduism, Islam or Christianity, must not permit ourselves complacency about the religion which we affirm. Hideous things have been done in the name of religion. Muslim rule has its murderous aspects, the sword has often been an instrument of policy in Israel and the Church itself has committed untold cruelties in order, so it was believed, to demolish heresy and to secure assent. Dear God, we cry for mercy and we need to know where mercy can be found. Blessed are the merciful.

The Bible Society concordance makes explicit what is implicit in the work of all translators. Sometimes one English word has to do service for several words of the original language. Sometimes one word in the original language can only be made intelligible in its context by the use of several English words. For the benefit of those who do not have the appropriate Greek or Hebrew concordances to work with I will try to unpack the problem so far as it relates to the word 'merciful'. No commentary is likely to be convincing unless this preliminary work has been done.

The word most often used to convey the idea of 'mercy' or 'merciful' in the Hebrew Scriptures is extremely common in the Old Testament. In the Psalms alone it occurs over one hundred and twenty times. That is apparent enough even in the English versions though the translators are not wholly consistent; they sometimes use the words loving kindness, goodness, good deeds. But there is another Hebrew word which is often rendered into English with the word 'mercy'; it is almost synonymous but not quite. It is a word derived from a root meaning 'womb' and carries with it an extra emotional tone sometimes translated in the English version as 'tender mercy' or 'compassion'. Whereas, therefore, we have been able to establish a fairly exact meaning for some of the Beatitudes we are not going to be able to do so this time simply on the basis of a study of the words. The original words in the Hebrew convey a whole range of meaning tied up with the essential relationship of men to other men. So much indeed is implied by the form of the Beatitude – God's mercy to us is inseparable from our mercy to others. The words therefore quoted under the word 'kind' in the concordance suggest more than a series of unrelated 'virtues' but rather a conspectus of the good life lived in accordance with the will and the nature of God Himself. This is indeed a large subject and we shall have to be prepared to take a large view of it.

The Greek version of the Old Testament, the Septuagint, is reasonably consistent in its translation of the Hebrew original. The same Greek word appears in the New Testament where in its various forms it is fairly common – over fifty times. But in this instance statistics about usage do not do justice to the prominence of the theme in the apostolic writings. The most striking evocation of the theme is to be found in St. Matthew 18: 21–35:

Then Peter came to Jesus and asked, 'Lord, how many times shall I forgive my brother when he sins against me? Up to seven times?' Jesus answered, 'I tell you, not seven times, but seventy-seven times.

'Therefore, the kingdom of heaven is like a king who wanted to settle accounts with his servants. As he began the settlement, a man who owed him ten thousand talents was brought to him. Since he was not able to pay, the master ordered that he and his wife and his children and all that he had be sold to repay the debt.

'The servant fell on his knees before him. "Be patient with me," he begged, "and I will pay back everything." The servant's master took pity on him, cancelled the debt and let him go.

'But when the servant went out, he found one of his fellow-servants who owed him a hundred denarii. He grabbed him and began to choke him. "Pay back what you owe me!" he demanded.

'His fellow-servant fell to his knees and begged him, "Be patient with me, and I will pay you back."

'But he refused. Instead, he went off and had the man thrown into prison until he could pay the debt. When the other servants saw what had happened, they were greatly distressed and went and told their master everything that had happened.

'Then the master called the servant in. "You wicked servant," he said, "I cancelled all that debt of yours because you begged me to. Shouldn't you have had mercy on your fellow-servant just as I had on you?" In anger his master turned him over to the jailers until he should pay back all he owed.

'This is how my heavenly Father will treat each of you unless you forgive your brother from your heart.'

Like many of Our Lord's parables this one has a long fuse. I have read it and have heard it read time without number. I have lavished academic time on the issues raised by it, but the moment came when I found myself convicted by it – here was I, secretly angry, critical of a fellow human being, demanding my rights, taking as it were my fellow-servant by the throat. I was under judgment and in danger of eternal punishment unless I was prepared to forgive my brother from my heart. So lavish is God's mercy to us in the provision of our needs and the forgiveness of our sins that we are under obligation to forgive our brother not just seven times but seventy-seven times.

A similar point is made in the parable of the Pharisee and the Publican:

To some who were confident of their own righteousness and looked down on everybody else, Jesus told this parable;

'Two men went up to the temple to pray, one a Pharisee and the other a tax collector. The Pharisee stood up and prayed about himself; "God, I thank you that I am not like other men – robbers, evildoers, adulterers – or even like this tax collector. I fast twice a week and give a tenth of all I get."

But the tax collector stood at a distance. He would not even look up to heaven, but beat his breast and said, "God, have mercy on me, a sinner."

I tell you that this man, rather than the other, went home justified before God. For everyone who exalts himself will be humbled, and he who humbles himself will be exalted.' (Luke 18: 9–14)

The point is similar but not the same. This parable is concerned primarily with our relationship with God rather than with men. The trouble with the Pharisee was that he was trapped in a system which he himself had made; in his enthusiasm for the Law and his diligent application of it to everyday life he had forgotten that he was still a sinner in need of forgiveness. The tax collector on the other hand knew that he had no claim on God; he was a flagrant rebel against the Law of his people, he was a man consumed with a desire for money at any cost, he had no doubt been responsible for the deprivation or even the ruin of some of his victims. He was a sinner and he knew it and yet he went down to his house justified. In the parable of the Good Samaritan, so familiar as not to need quotation, I ask you to observe how it ends:

Which of these three do you think was a neighbour to the man who fell into the hands of the robbers? The expert in the law replied, 'The one who had mercy on him.' Jesus told him, 'go and do likewise.' (Luke 10: 36-37)

It would not be too much to say that the idea of God's mercy to men and the need of our mercy to each other occupies quite a disproportionate space (if we look at it in that way) in the teaching of Christ. The so-called parable of the Prodigal Son might better be interpreted as the parable of the merciful father. The parable of Dives and Lazarus is as much about the rich man's failure to concern himself with the poor man's plight, as it is about the rewards and punishments in the next life. The parable of the Lost Sheep tells us something about lost sheep but it tells us even more about the consuming mercy and compassion of the Shepherd (Luke 15: 4-6). Twice Jesus quotes a saying from Hosea – 'Go and learn what this means: "I desire mercy, not sacrifice."' (Matthew 9:13. 12:7)

This Beatitude therefore is more fully represented in Our Lord's teaching than any of the others; mercy is a subject very near to His heart and He never tires of speaking of it. The same emphasis is to be observed in St. Paul and I quote a catena of sayings almost at random to illustrate the point:

I will have mercy on whom I have mercy and I will have compassion on whom I have compassion. (Romans 9: 15)

I tell you that Christ has become a servant of the Jews on behalf of God's truth, to confirm the promises made to the patriarchs so that the Gentiles may glorify God for His mercy. (Romans 15: 8-9)

Because of His great love for us, God, who is rich in mercy, made us alive with Christ even when we were dead in transgressions – it is by grace you have been saved. (Ephesians 2: 4, 5)

Grace, mercy and peace from God the Father and Christ

Jesus Our Lord. (1 Timothy 1: 2; 2 Timothy 1: 2; Titus 1: 4)

But perhaps more impressive than the mere assemblage of texts is his personal experience of mercy, expressed pre-eminently in 1 Timothy 1: 15–17.

Here is a trustworthy saying that deserves full acceptance: Christ Jesus came into the world to save sinners – of whom I am the worst. But for that very reason I was shown mercy so that in me, the worst of sinners, Christ Jesus might display his unlimited patience as an example for those who would believe in him and receive eternal life. Now to the King eternal, immortal, invisible, the only God, be honour and glory for ever and ever. Amen.

A whole universe of feeling lies behind that poignant utterance. If ever there was a man conscious of the mercy of God, for whom it became the linchpin of his faith and ministry, it was St. Paul. Had he not after all persecuted the Church of Christ? Had he not stood by as the first martyr was stoned to death? Had he not resisted the claims of Christ upon his life until it was nearly too late? He speaks of mercy often enough in the Epistles and in the Acts of the Apostles. That was no accident – he was a man vividly alive with gratitude for what God in Christ had done for him who deserved no mercy. God had had mercy on him; the least he could do was to offer that mercy to all men. The mercy of God was the mainspring of his mission to the Gentiles. It is sometimes suggested that St. Paul shows himself little aware of the teaching of Christ that has come down to us in the Gospels. That is, in a technical sense, true, but there is no doubt that he had absorbed this aspect of Our Lord's teaching or at least discovered it as the result of his experience on the Damascus Road.

You will be accustomed by now to look to the Old Testament for the distant origins of many of the dominant ideas of the New Testament. Jesus was a Jew brought up in a Jewish home, taught in a synagogue school; the Old

Testament was His Bible as it had been for millions of his
fellow countrymen. Where did He learn about mercy in
that book, dominated as it often seems to be by war,
cruelties, assassinations and imprisonments, battle cries
and shouts for vengeance? Here is a passage from the Song
of Moses after the crossing of the Red Sea:

> Then Moses and the Israelites sang this song to the Lord:
> 'I will sing to the Lord,
> for he is highly exalted.
> The horse and its rider
> he has hurled into the sea,
> The Lord is my strength and my song;
> he has become my salvation . . .
>
> Who among the gods is like you, O Lord?
> Who is like you –
> majestic in holiness,
> awesome in glory
> working wonders?
> You stretched out your right hand
> and the earth swallowed them.
>
> In your unfailing love you will lead
> the people you have redeemed.
> In your strength you will guide them
> to your holy dwelling.' (Exodus 15: 1, 2, 11–13)

'Majestic in holiness, awesome in glory, working wonders'
– yes indeed, but not much trace of mercy for those who
perished in the waters and for those who mourned them
back at home. But we have to learn to live with the fact that
Israel was a subject people in a savage world where war
was an instrument of policy and massacre a commonplace. We are in no better situation. If I had known the
Song of Moses I could have sung it in Burma when facing,
as I thought, the prospect of an almost interminable war I
heard the news of the Japanese surrender after the
immolation of Hiroshima and Nagasaki.

There are other notes to be heard in the Old Testament symphony, muted perhaps, but instinct with a sense of the mercy of God, later to become the dominant theme of Our Lord's life and teaching. The psalmists never tire of singing of the mercy of God and there is one book in particular which, whilst firmly bedded in the Old Covenant, wonderfully prepares the way for the New Covenant. The Book of Hosea is one of the most obscure books in the Old Testament, as you will see for yourself if you glance at the number of variant readings in the margin. The true text in some places is irrecoverable and even when we have what we believe to be the right text, it is by no means easy to interpret. But for all its obscurities the main message, at least, is clear. It is the message of this Beatitude – blessed are the merciful for they will be shown mercy.

Scholarly opinion is divided as to the circumstances surrounding Hosea's life. It would appear that either Hosea married Gomer, a temple prostitute, and sought to reclaim her, or he married Gomer who bore him two children but then left him for a series of adulterous relationships. Hosea's understanding of God's relationship with Israel was deeply coloured by this personal experience of betrayal. We shall not be surprised therefore to find that the word for mercy occurs six times within the comparatively narrow compass of his book. Here is a typical passage:

Say of your brothers, 'My people', and of your sisters, 'My loved one'.
Rebuke your mother, rebuke her,
for she is not my wife,
and I am not her husband.
Let her remove the adulterous look from her face
and the unfaithfulness from between her breasts.
Otherwise I will strip her naked
and make her as bare as on the day she was born;
I will make her like a desert,

turn her into a parched land,
and slay her with thirst.
I will not show my love to her children,
Because they are the children of adultery.
Their mother has been unfaithful
and has conceived them in disgrace.
She said, 'I will go after my lovers,
who give me my food and my water,
my wool and my linen, my oil and my drink.'
Therefore I will block her path with thornbushes;
I will wall her in so that she cannot find her way.
She will chase after her lovers but not catch them;
she will look for them but not find them.
Then she will say,
'I will go back to my husband as at first,
for then I was better off than now.'
She has not acknowledged that I was the one
who gave her the grain, the new wine and oil,
who lavished on her the silver and gold
which they used for Baal...
I will punish her for the days
she burned incense to the Baals;
she decked herself with rings and jewellery,
and went after her lovers,
but me she forgot,'
declares the Lord.
'Therefore I am now going to allure her,
I will lead her into the desert
and speak tenderly to her.' (Hosea 2: 1-8, 13, 14)

Like any other man, Hosea bitterly resented his wife's betrayal, her disregard of all the good things he had provided for her, her neglect of the children she had borne him. But then he found another voice whispering in his heart, and it was the voice of God reminding him of God's patience with the people of Israel whom he had rescued from slavery in Egypt, sustained in the wilderness and planted in Canaan, but who now disdained the covenant. They had committed adultery with other gods and forgotten what God had done for them. But observe, as

Paul puts it, 'the goodness and... long-suffering' (Romans 2:4, R.V.). So Hosea's own life had proved to be a parable of God's sense of outrage at his people's betrayal but also his everlasting mercy. Blessed are the merciful for they will be shown mercy. It is the thought of God's mercy to him and to his people which engenders in his own heart a new attitude towards the errant Gomer:

> The Lord said to me, 'Go, show your love to your wife again, though she is loved by another and is an adulteress. Love her as the Lord loves the Israelites, though they turn to other gods and love the sacred raisin-cakes.'
> So I bought her for fifteen shekels of silver and about a homer and a lethek of barley. Then I told her, 'You are to live with me for many days; you must not be a prostitute or be intimate with any man, and I will live with you.' (Hosea 3:1-3)

Even in the pages of the New Testament there is hardly a more poignant and moving expression of the great truth that lies behind the Beatitude, eight hundred years before that Beatitude took the form with which we are familiar in the teaching of Our Lord and in the tradition of the Church. Any man or woman who has been subjected to the same treatment as the prophet Hosea will know how he felt and may discover by God's mercy the grace to forgive – seventy times seven. If ever there was a message for embittered nations and ravaged lives it is the call to be merciful as our heavenly Father is merciful.

In each of the preceding chapters I have tried to isolate and identify a situation in the world of Our Lord's own day which called forth and gave shape to a particular Beatitude. This was a necessary exercise if only to give particularity to a saying which might otherwise become vague and unattached. Thus, the saying about the poor in spirit derives at least part of its significance from the fact that a group calling themselves 'the poor' actually existed. The meek are contrasted with the violent men who would take the kingdom by storm. Those who hunger and thirst after righteousness are compared and contrasted with the Pharisees who had their own formula for achieving it.

Did the saying about the merciful have some special meaning for the man who uttered it and for those who heard it?

To the best of my knowledge no such group as 'the merciful' existed. In a world dominated by cruelties of one kind or another Our Lord does not seem to have had any particular target in mind. But there was a mental scenery in which both Our Lord and His hearers inevitably shared even if they were not always conscious of it. That mental scenery is known to historians as Hellenism. It followed in the train of Alexander's conquests dating from the year 336 B.C. and it had a pervasive influence throughout the civilised world of which Palestine was a part. It constituted a persistent problem for the Jewish people, especially for those who lived in the Greek cities of the Ancient World. It has to be said that there were far more Jews outside Palestine than inside it, and large Jewish communities existed in Egypt and Greece and Rome. They had an uncomfortable choice to make. Hellenism offered seductive possibilities – a highly sophisticated educational system which included some of the great universities of the world, a culture rich in art and drama, music and poetry, dominated by the Homeric epics as our English culture has been dominated by Shakespeare. And then there were the games, gymnasiums, the great public shows, the exciting religious festivals.

Everything about the Jews had set them apart from this throbbing life by which they were surrounded. They were exceedingly strict about diet and this debarred them from easy social intercourse through their neighbours. They refused to work on Saturdays, which made it difficult for them to reach high rank in the army for example, or to work for the Civil Service. They were subject to the stringent regulations of their law which excluded the worship or even the possession of images. They were a people set apart, living in their own ghettos, maintaining their own way of life.

Inevitably there were some, often the ablest amongst them, who could not tolerate this exclusive stance and carved out for themselves a career in and enjoyed the fruits of the Greek way of life. St. Paul's father sent him to Jerusalem for his university education. Less strict fathers sent their sons to the great university at Tarsus as a gateway, so they hoped, to a dazzling academic or public career. But even in the homeland Jews were not quite immune to the attractions of Hellenism. Even there they lived in a cosmopolitan society and you will have noticed that some of Our Lord's disciples had Greek names. Even a 'master of Israel' was known to Our Lord and his disciples as Nicodemus, a Greek word meaning 'conqueror of the people'. There was no way that the Jews as a race could be wholly isolated from the civilisation of which they were a part.[2] But Hellenism was not just a social, intellectual system. It was a religious system as well and the Christian Church has always hesitated uneasily between accommodation with it and all-out war against it. The battle is by no means over even today.

At its best Hellenism was a profoundly attractive and satisfying concept of culture, philosophy and religion closely interwoven. It looked back to Plato for its inspiration, and Platonic schools in various guises and under various leaders lived on long into the Christian era. What the Church is today is the product of an uneasy alliance between Hebraic and Hellenic models of thought; even the development of Christian doctrine has sometimes been described as 'the acute Hellenisation of Christianity'. So, we have to ask a basic question – what is it in Hellenism that makes it compatible or incompatible with Judaism and its successor, Christianity? Plato, says Dr. Nygren,[3]

has achieved in his doctrine of forms a synthesis between

Hellenic rationalism and oriental mysticism ... in Plato we do not get philosophy in the modern sense of an abstract critical study, but a philosophy which is also a world outlook constructed largely on a religious basis; it might be said that it is a doctrine of salvation as much as a philosophy, for we constantly hear the exhortation to take thought for our soul's health. The ancient world drew no sharp line between religion and philosophy; both had a message to give concerning the attainment of the true and the blessed life.

Both Hellenism and Christianity (and the Beatitudes in particular) have a message to give concerning the attainment of the true and the blessed life, but the way of salvation is different. For Plato and his followers 'salvation means the deliverance of the soul from the bondage of sense and her return to the heavenly home to which she belongs'.[4] Thus, the way is seen as a steep ascent from the world of sense to the world of reality, a long pilgrimage, rewarded in the end by the beatific vision, which was to be undertaken only by strenuous athletes of the spirit prepared for hardship and self-denial. If that does not sound incompatible with the Christian faith as you understand it, that is some indication how far our Christian faith has been influenced by the Hellenic view of life. In that view God stands at the end of a process, is the object and goal of man's desiring, that to which all creation moves; God is by definition far off, only to be approached by severe ascetic exercises which call for heroic effort on behalf of the man who seeks thereby salvation. Dr. Kirk, formerly Bishop of Oxford, pays his own tribute to the Platonic view of life in his book *The Vision of God*[5], but he would have been the first to recognise that there is a difference. The difference is this: for the Greeks, God was the god of Plato, remote in the heavens, inviting adoration but untouched with the infirmities of men, distant from the battles on earth. He is an idea in the mind, haunting them but not embracing them; he does not run out of his house to greet the returning prodigal; he waits inside until the prodigal has paid his debt. The God of the Hebrews, the God of Abraham, Isaac and Jacob is one who takes the initiative. He summons Abraham to a long journey, He procures a wife for Isaac, He meets Jacob at the ford. The great men of the Old Testament are not men in love with an idea or in pursuit of blessedness, they are not given to elaborate ascetic exercises; they are men to whom God has spoken, for whom God provides. He is nearer than hands and feet, closer than breathing; He is not the end of a 'long search', He is the beginning of it.

All this may seem far removed from the fifth Beatitude – but not so. Our Lord and His disciples lived in a world that was dominated by these teachings of Plato; they even infiltrated the sacred literature of the Hebrew people. The so-called 'Wisdom of Solomon', now a part of the Apocrypha, owes little to Solomon but a lot to Plato. It is thought to be a product of the first or second century B.C. and reflects a view popular in some circles of Jewish life. It is a beautiful book, but it contains sentiments far removed from the downright, earthy theology of the Old Testament, e.g.

> But the souls of the righteous are in the hand of God, and there shall no torment touch them.
> In the sight of the unwise they seemed to die: and their departure is taken for misery.
> And their going from us to be utter destruction: but they are in peace.
> For though they be punished in the sight of men, yet is their hope full of immortality.
> And having been a little chastised, they shall be greatly rewarded: for God proved them, and found them worthy for himself. (Wisdom of Solomon 3: 1-5)

> For I was a witty child, and had a good spirit,
> Yea rather, being good, I came into a body undefiled. (Wisdom of Solomon 8: 19-20)

> For the corruptible body presseth down the soul, and the earthy tabernacle weigheth down the mind that museth upon many things.
> And hardly do we guess aright at things that are upon earth, and with labour do we find the things that are before us: but the things that are in heaven who hath searched out?
> And thy counsel who hath known, except thou give wisdom, and send thy Holy Spirit from above?
> For so the ways of them which lived on the earth were reformed, and men were taught the things that are pleasing unto them, and were saved through wisdom. (Wisdom of Solomon 9: 15–18)

I have quoted passages which have achieved naturalisation even within the liturgy of the Church, and are sometimes to be heard on special occasions. But they bear witness 'to the extent to which Judaism had been open to Hellenistic influence before the arrival of Christianity'.[6] To look at it in a modern context, not many of my readers will be familiar with the works of Kierkegaard, but we live now in an intellectual world profoundly influenced by him.

Against this unconscious background the Beatitude stands out like a great rock in a desert sand. It proclaims (to return once more to the Bible Society concordance) God is 'merciful, compassionate, concerned, considerate, friendly, gentle, gracious, pitiful, sympathetic, tender'. He is no great potentate sitting at the end of time in some cosmic throne room waiting for the weary travellers to arrive. He is the good shepherd, merciful to struggling mankind, leading them into fresh pastures, guiding them through dark valleys, spreading a table in the wilderness from which to eat. He is not Eros, the faint image that haunts the human heart, but Agape, rich in compassion and mercy, pouring out His life in Christ for the sake of those who would never otherwise find Him or know Him. It is the love of God which has been shed abroad in the hearts of those who believe in Him (Romans 5: 5) – not our love for Him, I hasten to explain, but His love for us. It is the love of God for us which provides the pattern for our love for our fellow human beings:

> Love is patient, love is kind. It does not envy, it does not boast, it is not proud. It is not rude, it is not self-seeking, it is not easily angered, it keeps no record of wrongs. Love does not delight in evil but rejoices with the truth. It always protects, always trusts, always hopes, always perseveres. (1 Corinthians 13: 4–7)

It is because God is merciful that we have to be merciful. It is because God is merciful that we are capable of mercy. God 'declares His almighty power most chiefly in showing mercy and pity' (B.C.P. Collect for Trinity 11). 'It is His nature always to have mercy' (B.C.P. Prayer of Humble Access).

'Blessed are the merciful for they have the merciful for their Lord'.[7]

## Chapter 10

# BLESSED ARE THE PURE IN HEART FOR THEY WILL SEE GOD

True to our practice throughout this book so far, I take first of all the context of this saying. Does it bear upon a particular problem in Our Lord's day? Is it a response to a particular issue in the minds of His disciples or of those multitudes who heard His teaching from afar? Does it reflect some experience in His own life, some conflict perhaps with the religious authorities? The context of the saying in the world at large is well described in Dr. Kirk's book *The Vision of God*:[1]

> What is clear so far is that Christianity came into a world tantalised with the belief that some men at least had seen God, and had found in the vision the sum of human happiness; a world aching with the hope that the same vision was attainable by all. Men came into the Church assured that there, if anywhere, they would 'see God'; and they brought with them all the diverse conceptions of theology and conduct with which the thought was invested in non-Christian circles. Their quest was primarily a selfish one; their motive to secure for themselves, either here or hereafter, an all-absorbing religious experience.

Many were the practitioners who ministered to this need – the devotees of the 'mystery religions', the followers of a prophet here or a magician there, the seekers for divine

wisdom, philosophers in pursuit of the intellectual elixir
of life. So the phrase would have meant something,
however vague, to the well-educated in Our Lord's
company, and something, however extravagant, to the
cosmopolitan crowds which milled around him in His
native Galilee.

If the Beatitudes were, as is sometimes supposed, texts
upon which a series of sermons were constructed there
would have been those in the crowds who would have been
eagerly waiting for the sermon; and were, as Dr. Kirk puts
it, evidence of 'a world aching with hope'. But there might
have been those in the crowd or in the more select circle of
Our Lord's immediate friends for whom the saying would
have reverberated along chords already familiar to them. It
would be a mistake to assume that the inhabitants of
Galilee were unfamiliar with the thought-pattern of the
other great civilisations of the world. Most of the Jews,
most of the time, lived cheek-by-jowl with their Gentile
neighbours and could hardly have failed to be influenced
by the thought, the culture, the arts and the education of
the Ancient World. More Jews, it is said, lived in
Alexandria at the time of Our Lord than in Palestine, and
one of them was certainly contemporary with Jesus of
Nazareth. His name was Philo (20 B.C.–A.D. 50); he was a
member of a prosperous, priestly family in Alexandria. He
was a prolific author and his influence in the Jewish and
Gentile world was immense. The so-called 'Wisdom of
Solomon' in the Apocrypha may well have been
influenced by him. He was as Dr. Kirk says 'athirst for
God', and I quote one of the most exalted passages in his
writing:

> I am not ashamed to confess that which has befallen me a
> thousand times. I have set myself down according to my wont
> to write upon the principles of philosophy. I have seen clearly
> what I wish to say. Yet my mind has remained blank and sterile
> and I have abandoned the attempt, cursing the impotence of

my mind but amazed at the might of Him who is, who at His will doth open and close the womb of the soul. At other times, coming empty-handed to my work I have suddenly been filled. In some strange way ideas have poured in upon me from above like rain or snow; I knew no more the place where I sat, my company, myself – nay even what I said or wrote.

It is likely that the circles in which Nicodemus, for example, lived would have been well familiar with the writings of their great contemporary in Alexandria. What may have surprised Nicodemus was that he should have been told by Jesus that he would need to be born again if he wished to see the kingdom of God (John 3: 3). He might well have thought that there were other ways, e.g. by prophetic ecstasy or by philosophical reflection, but the Beatitude would not have been meaningless to him.

Philo provided a diet for the few; the many would have been influenced more by the traditions of their fathers as they were represented in the religion of Galilee and Judah. Going to the temple would have been a recognised formula for seeing God. The study of the Torah was thought to open the gates of heaven and reveal the Lord on His throne. 'He who haunts the synagogue and the school-house, these are the men to whom the presence will manifest itself' – a sentence which is echoed in a remark by the great Christian scholar Sir Edwin Hoskyns when he said of his own studies that often enough he had begun with his head in a lexicon and ended at the throne of God. So those who haunted the synagogue or the schoolhouse in Our Lord's day would have been perfectly familiar with the concept even if they lacked the experience of 'seeing God'.

Nearer at hand to the honest seeker after God would have been the sacred Scriptures themselves:

The Old Testament scintillates with sublime examples of men whose communion with God was a thing of intensest reality to them, and whose conviction of the nearness to the divine was beyond the slightest cavil.[2]

The most marked examples are to be found in the Prophets and I quote one of the most famous of them all, the account of Isaiah's call to be a prophet:

> In the year that King Uzziah died, I saw the Lord seated on a throne, high and exalted, and the train of his robe filled the temple. Above him were seraphs, each with six wings. With two wings they covered their faces, with two they covered their feet, and with two they were flying. And they were calling to one another:
> 'Holy, holy, holy is the Lord Almighty:
> the whole earth is full of his glory.'
> At the sound of their voices the doorposts and thresholds shook and the temple was filled with smoke.
> 'Woe to me!' I cried. 'I am ruined! For I am a man of unclean lips, and I live among a people of unclean lips, and my eyes have seen the King, the Lord Almighty.'
> Then one of the seraphs flew to me with a live coal in his hand, which he had taken with tongs from the altar. With it he touched my mouth and said, 'See, this has touched your lips, your guilt is taken away and your sin atoned for.'
> Then I heard the voice of the Lord saying, 'Whom shall I send? And who will go for us?'
> And I said, 'Here I am! Send me!' (Isaiah 6: 1–8)

This passage will stand for many similar experiences recorded in the prophetic writings and I therefore permit myself a few comments on it. The solemn reading of it in church on high days and holy days does not always illuminate its meaning. King Uzziah had been one of the great kings of Israel, his reign marked by strong government and secure borders. Isaiah would not have been the only one to tremble at the thought of what would happen after his death. It was in that moment that Isaiah saw the Lord high and lifted up on His throne – a plain message that the real security of Israel lay not in the achievements of their kings, however great, but in the loving providence of the God who ruled over all. It was a life-transforming vision of the universal reign of the God of Israel. But observe (and this is common to most of the

prophets) that Isaiah did not relish his vision. It was part
of a routine visit to the temple and was wholly unexpected.
So far from being elevated by the vision he had received, he
felt chastened and afraid, for in the light of that vision he
knew himself to be a man of unclean lips; he was 'ruined'.
Observe also that the vision was not a reward for long
service or the climax of a long process of intellectual or
moral pursuit; rather it came to a young man who had not
been seeking it and who was deeply perturbed at the
thought of what it might entail for the rest of his life. The
vision constituted not a reward but a command. The
essence of the vision of God in the Hebrew tradition, as
distinct from almost every other tradition which nurtured
this hope, is that it comes to people wholly unprepared for
it, by the sheer grace of God who will reveal Himself to
whom He will reveal Himself and call to His service those
whom He will call. There is no way that we can command
or engineer a vision; we can only respond to it.

The vision, whether it be of a Philo or of an Isaiah, was
not without precedent in the early traditions of Israel. The
beginning of all Hebrew religion is associated with the
vision to Abraham:

After this, the word of the Lord came to Abram in a vision:
'Do not be afraid, Abram.
I am your shield,
your very great reward.'
   But Abram said, 'O Sovereign Lord, what can you give me
since I remain childless and the one who will inherit my estate
is Eliezer of Damascus?' And Abram said, 'You have given me
no children; so a servant in my household will be my heir.'
   Then the word of the Lord came to him: 'This man will not
be your heir, but a son coming from your own body will be
your heir.' He took him outside and said, 'Look up to the
heavens and count the stars – if indeed you can count them.'
Then he said to him, 'So shall your offspring be.' (Genesis 15:
1–5)

What is interesting about this particular vision is that it is immediately followed by an horrific experience of the same living God:

> As the sun was setting, Abram fell into a deep sleep, and a thick and dreadful darkness came over him. Then the Lord said to him, 'Know for certain that your descendants will be strangers in a country not their own, and they will be enslaved and ill-treated four hundred years. But I will punish the nation they serve as slaves, and afterwards they will come out with great possessions. You, however, will go to your fathers in peace and be buried at a good old age. In the fourth generation your descendants will come back here, for the sin of the Amorites has not yet reached its full measure.' (Genesis 15: 12–16)

Thus, early on in the tradition of Israel the vision of God is represented not only by ecstasy and delight but by horror and darkness – certainly not to be sought for its own sake, a burden rather than a privilege, a devastation of human life rather than an enhancement of it. The same pattern is to be observed in the visionary experiences of Jacob. Afraid of the wrath of his brother, Jacob leaves home and sets off to the territory of his uncle, Laban the Aramaean. This is what happened to him on the way:

> Jacob left Beersheba and set out for Haran. When he reached a certain place, he stopped for the night because the sun had set. Taking one of the stones there, he put it under his head and lay down to sleep. He had a dream in which he saw a stairway resting on the earth, with its top reaching to heaven, and the angels of God were ascending and descending on it.
> There above it stood the Lord, and he said: 'I am the Lord, the God of your father Abraham and the God of Isaac. I will give you and your descendants the land on which you are lying. Your descendants will be like the dust of the earth, and you will spread out to the west and to the east, to the north and to the south. All peoples on earth will be blessed through you and your offspring. I am with you and will watch over you wherever you go, and I will bring you back to this land. I will not leave you until I have done what I have promised you.'
> When Jacob awoke from his sleep, he thought, 'Surely the

Lord is in this place, and I was not aware of it.' He was afraid and said, 'How awesome is this place! This is none other than the house of God; this is the gate of heaven.' (Genesis 28: 10-17)

'The gate of heaven' – a welcome vision for a man who at that moment appeared to have no earthly hopes. But many years later on his way back to his homeland he has another vision when faced with an unwelcome reunion with his brother Esau:

> That night Jacob got up and took his two wives, his two maidservants and his eleven sons and crossed the ford of the Jabbok. After he had sent them across the stream, he sent over all his possessions. So Jacob was left alone, and a man wrestled with him till daybreak. When the man saw that he could not overpower him, he touched the socket of Jacob's hip so that his hip was wrenched as he wrestled with the man. Then the man said, 'Let me go, for it is daybreak.'
>
> But Jacob replied, 'I will not let you go unless you bless me.' The man asked him, 'What is your name?' 'Jacob,' he answered.
>
> Then the man said, 'Your name will no longer be Jacob, but Israel, because you have struggled with God and with men and have overcome.'
>
> Jacob said, 'Please tell me your name'. But he replied, 'Why do you ask my name?' Then he blessed him there.
>
> So Jacob called the place Peniel, saying, 'It is because I saw God face to face, and yet my life was spared.'
>
> Then the sun rose above him as he passed Peniel, and he was limping because of his hip. Therefore to this day the Israelites do not eat the tendon attached to the socket of the hip, because the socket of Jacob's hip was touched near the tendon. (Genesis 32: 22-32)

No 'gate of heaven' this time but a dark night of the soul, bitter struggle and permanent injury.

The same ambivalence is to be observed in the life of Moses. His first vision of the burning bush constituted a summons to be the liberator of his people, but the second is of a different character altogether. In an obscure verse it is said that 'at a lodging place on the way the Lord met Moses and was about to kill him.' (Exodus 4: 24). It is as if a man who is exposed to the light in due course must also be exposed to the darkness, and this has been a feature of Jewish and Christian mysticism ever since.

These early experiences of Israel are vividly revived in the experience of the early Church. Paul's vision on the Damascus road was wholly unsought and in the first instance thoroughly destructive; he continued his journey to Damascus blind and nearly dead: like Isaiah his vision was not a reward for long perseverence but a summons to unwelcome activity at the behest of the God and Father of Our Lord Jesus Christ. But Paul's vision would not itself have been sufficient had not Ananias responded to a deeply disturbing vision of his own:

> In Damascus there was a disciple named Ananias. The Lord called to him in a vision, 'Ananias!'
>
> 'Yes, Lord,' he answered.
>
> The Lord told him, 'Go to the house of Judas on Straight Street and ask for a man from Tarsus named Saul, for he is praying. In a vision he has seen a man named Ananias come and place his hands on him to restore his sight.'
>
> 'Lord', Ananias answered, 'I have heard many reports about this man and all the harm he has done to your saints in Jerusalem. And he has come here with authority from the chief priests to arrest all who call on your name.'
>
> But the Lord said to Ananias, 'Go! This man is my chosen instrument to carry my name before the Gentiles and their kings and before the people of Israel. I will show him how much he must suffer for my name.'
>
> Then Ananias went to the house and entered it. Placing his hands on Saul, he said, 'Brother Saul, the Lord – Jesus, who appeared to you on the road as you were coming here – has sent me so that you may see again and be filled with the Holy Spirit.' Immediately, something like scales fell from Saul's eyes, and he could see again. He got up and was baptised. (Acts 9: 10–18)

The aim of this chapter so far has been to illustrate that

Our Lord in this Beatitude is addressing men and women who are already thoroughly familiar with the concept of 'seeing God'. But perhaps they had grown content with the vision of God as something distinctly of the past, associated with great moments in the history of Israel. Perhaps they no longer went to the synagogue or to the temple with a lively expectation of seeing God. It was now a part of the tradition to be treated with loving recollection, not to be emulated. For them now, at best, it was a matter of keeping the law as best they could, attending the synagogue as often as they were able and rejoicing in the traditions of their people as in a distant past. Much the same could be said of the Church. We read about visions but we do not expect them. We observe how God guided men to unthinkable acts of heroism and service, we hear occasionally how humble men and women of our own day have dreams and see visions; but we keep ourselves to ourselves, we tread a well-trodden path, we do not, so it seems, meet God on the way. But we are left with this strange disturbing saying – 'Blessed are the pure in heart for they shall see God.' The words glide over the mind; they are amongst the most familiar words in the English language. But what do they mean?

Dr. Kirk's book *The Vision of God* has as its sub-heading 'The Christian Doctrine of the Summum Bonum'. Put another way, it means that the only life worth living is the life that has for its objective the vision of God. But as we have seen already, even within the pages of Scripture the phrase means something different to different people in different ages, and its meaning will determine the means by which that vision is sought.

One way of looking at the Summum Bonum, espoused by the Neoplatonists and represented par excellence in the writings of Plotinus (*c*. 205–270 A.D.), perceives the vision of God in terms of abstraction from the world and is characteristically expressed in this extract from the writings of Plotinus:

Caught up in ecstasy tranquil and God-possessed he (the mystic) enjoyed an imperturbable calm; shut up in his proper essence he inclined not to either side, he turned not even to himself; he was in state of perfect stability. If then a man sees himself become one with the One, he has in himself a likeness of the One, and if he passes out of himself as an image to its archetype he has reached the end of his journey. And when he comes down from his vision he can again awaken the virtue that is in him, and seeing himself fitly adorned in every part he can again mount upward through virtue to spirit and through wisdom to the One itself. Such is the life of Gods and of God-like and blessed men; a liberation from all earthly bonds, a life that takes no pleasure in earthly things, a flight of the alone to the alone.

Few could altogether resist the charm of a life lived with this objective in view amidst the sadnesses and disasters of our earthly life. But, as Georgia Harkness says, 'to withdraw from all earthly entanglements and seek after a life that takes no pleasure in earthly things is not the good life as Jesus understood it. It has never been and ought never to become the dominant note in Christian mysticism.'[3] The fact remains, however, that this view of 'the only thing worth living for in this world' has been extremely influential in the life of the Church and perhaps it is necessary to say why.

After Paul's sermon in Athens, Luke records that 'A few men became followers of Paul and believed. Among them was Dionysius, a member of the Areopagus, also a woman named Damaris, and a number of others.' (Acts 17: 34). This Dionysius, otherwise unknown, achieved a certain fame in the course of fifth- and sixth-century controversies in the Church and his writings became embedded in the mystical tradition of the Church, achieving authority there because of his supposed association with the great Apostle himself. In fact, the writings ascribed to him are now known as the pseudo-Dionysian writings because there is little doubt that he is an author of the fifth century

indebted not to a secret deposit of knowledge acquired
from the great Apostle but to the Neoplatonists and to
Plotinus in particular. His kind of mysticism 'has never
been and ought never to become the dominant note in
Christian mysticism', but Georgia Harkness would be the
first to admit that it did in fact dominate mediaeval
theology and has remained the climate in which without
knowing it many have pursued the vision of God. This
comment does not deny the reality of their experience; they
did enjoy a 'flight of the alone to the alone', but it is
doubtful whether the Beatitude can be invoked in their
cause. The objective prescribes the means. If liberation
from all earthly bonds, a life that takes no pleasure in
earthly things is the only worthwhile objective, then it
follows that the mystical vision cannot but be associated
with a stern asceticism, as men and women seek to break
the bonds of their earthly appetites and desires, even if it
means sitting on a pillar in the desert or going without
food or living a life of savage deprivations. It is true that
Our Lord endured forty days in the wilderness, had
nowhere to lay his head and was dependent on the charity
of others, but He never exalted asceticism as a way of life
and acknowledged that, in contrast to St. John the Baptist,
He was regarded as a glutton and a wine-bibber, a man
altogether too fond of parties. Such rigours as He imposed
upon His apostles were rigours inseparable from the life
they were subsequently called to live in their ministry of
the Gospel. St. Paul did not go out of his way to invite
hardships; he simply encountered them and braved them
in pursuit of the apostolic mission he had received from
Christ. Georgia Harkness is right – the life that takes no
pleasure in earthly things is not a good life as Jesus
understood it. He Himself rejoiced in the natural world
and was obviously at home amidst the domestic felicities
of ordinary life. Other ways were available to Him in the
Judaean desert, in the settlements on the shores of the
Dead Sea, but He did not take them. We have therefore to
dismiss from our minds any such interpretation of this

Beatitude. Our only recourse is to do what we have invariably done in previous chapters – to try and establish the immediate context of the saying and thus to determine what it meant then before we seek to answer the question what it means now.

Let me begin therefore with the word itself – 'pure'. The word, as you will have learnt to expect by now, has a long history in both the Greek and the Hebrew language. We are accustomed to impart to the world 'pure' certain ethical and moral connotations, but neither the Greek nor the Hebrew word which lies behind it had any such connotation in the beginning. The word meant 'clean' rather than 'pure' and it is associated in the Ancient World with certain taboos connected with birth, death, sex life and totem animals. It is not surprising, therefore, that early cultic practice both in Israel and elsewhere laid great stress on washings, lustrations, symbolic baths.

Associated with the outward cleansing of the body was the preoccupation with diet and the prohibitions against the eating of unclean animals. These early taboos played a prominent part in the early life of Israel and came to be regulated and organised in a formidable array of legislation to which every Israelite by virtue of his faith was bound. Two aspects of Hebrew life mark them off from their neighbours and became a potent force in every society where the Jews rubbed shoulders with the Gentiles: the observance of the Sabbath, and the dietary and cleansing regulations. A corpse is unclean and excludes a person in contact with it from the inner courts of the temple. Samaritan women were regarded as unclean from childhood and could not be approached without risk of impurity. If a Jew buys a vessel from a Gentile he must cleanse it in accordance with detailed and specific regulations laid down for the purpose.[4] Life for the observant Jew was and still is an unremitting struggle to escape defilement and to remove it when unconsciously acquired.

The word 'pure' then in the Beatitude without the

qualification 'in heart' would have had a very plain
meaning to Our Lord's hearers. If they were hearing Him
for the first time they would have taken Him to mean that
He was insisting upon the most rigorous observance of the
laws of purity as a means of seeing God. But this obvious
meaning is excluded by other events in Our Lord's life
where He found Himself seriously at issue with His fellow
Rabbis on precisely this matter. His meeting with a
Samaritan woman at the well recorded in John 4 was a
clear infringement of the purity laws relating to Samari-
tans. It is sometimes supposed, and with good cause, that
the Parable of the Good Samaritan points the contrast
between the priest and the Levite bound by the purity laws
and the Samaritan who was not. Jesus made a practice of
eating with 'sinners', a technical term for describing those
who did not keep the Law in all its rigour and who were
excluded from full participation in the Jewish religion by
virtue of their trade or status. He insisted on touching a
leper (Mark 1: 41) which was utterly forbidden by the Law.
His most extended comment on this controversial issue is
reported in Mark 7: 14-23:

> Again Jesus called the crowd to him and said, 'Listen to me,
> everyone, and understand this. Nothing outside a man can
> make him "unclean" by going into him. Rather, it is what
> comes out of a man that makes him "unclean".'
> After he had left the crowd and entered the house, his
> disciples asked him about this parable. 'Are you so dull?' he
> asked. 'Don't you see that nothing that enters a man from the
> outside can make him "unclean"? For it doesn't go into his
> heart but into his stomach, and then out of his body.' (In
> saying this, Jesus declared all foods 'clean'.)
> He went on: 'What comes out of a man is what makes him
> "unclean". For from within, out of men's hearts, come evil
> thoughts, sexual immorality, theft, murder, adultery, greed,
> malice, deceit, lewdness, envy, slander, arrogance and folly.
> All these evils come from inside and make a man "unclean".'

The phrase 'in saying this Jesus declared all foods clean' is as it were in brackets representing Mark's own view of the significance of this discourse for the life of the early Church, and it shows how important the issue was. It is striking that immediately after this particular encounter He 'left that place and went to the vicinity of Tyre. He entered a house and did not want anyone to know it; yet he could not keep his presence secret' (Mark 7: 24). In so doing He infringed the Law by moving into unclean territory, staying in an unclean house and subsequently conversing with an unclean woman. So it was that in two very distinct characteristics of Jewish life He found Himself at odds with the official line – He challenged the regulations relating to the Sabbath and He overturned the huge body of Law relating to purity.

Not much imagination is required to see the importance of this issue in the life and mission of the early Church. The apostles were in the main observant Jews, reared in and loyal to the traditions of their fathers, keeping the Sabbath with exemplary care and avoiding at all costs contamination by unclean food or by unclean people. If their traditions had prevailed over the clear teaching of Our Lord there would have been no mission to the Gentiles; Christians would have remained firmly within the fold and would ultimately have expired as many another Jewish sect had done. The history of the world would have been different. But it required a vision to hammer this lesson home. I quote now from what with hindsight appears to be the record of one of the decisive battles of the Ancient World:

At Caesarea there was a man named Cornelius, a centurion in what was known as the Italian Regiment. He and all his family were devout and God-fearing; he gave generously to those in need and prayed to God regularly. One day at about three in the afternoon he had a vision. He distinctly saw an angel of God, who came to him and said, 'Cornelius!'

Cornelius stared at him in fear, 'What is it, Lord?' he asked. The angel answered, 'Your prayers and gifts to the poor have

come up as a memorial offering before God. Now send men to
Joppa to bring back a man named Simon who is called Peter.
He is staying with Simon the tanner, whose house is by the
sea.'

When the angel who spoke to him had gone, Cornelius
called two of his servants and a devout soldier who was one of
his attendants. He told them everything that had happened
and sent them to Joppa.

About noon the following day as they were approaching the
city, Peter went up on the roof to pray. He became hungry and
wanted something to eat, and while the meal was being
prepared, he fell into a trance. He saw heaven opened and
something like a large sheet being let down to earth by its four
corners. It contained all kinds of four-footed animals, as well
as reptiles of the earth and birds of the air. Then a voice told
him, 'Get up, Peter. Kill and eat.'

'Surely not, Lord!' Peter replied. 'I have never eaten
anything impure or unclean.'

The voice spoke to him a second time, 'Do not call anything
impure that God has made clean.'

This happened three times, and immediately the sheet was
taken back to heaven. While Peter was wondering about the
meaning of the vision, the men sent by Cornelius found out
where Simon's house was and stopped at the gate. They called
out, asking if Simon who was known as Peter was staying
there. While Peter was still thinking about the vision, the
Spirit said to him, 'Simon, three men are looking for you. So
get up and go downstairs. Do not hesitate to go with them, for I
have sent them.'

Peter went down and said to the men, 'I'm the one you're
looking for. Why have you come?'

The men replied, 'We have come from Cornelius the
centurion. He is a righteous and God-fearing man, who is
respected by all the Jewish people. A holy angel told him to
have you come to his house so that he could hear what you
have to say.' Then Peter invited the men into the house to be
his guests.

The next day Peter started out with them, and some of the
brothers from Joppa went along. The following day he arrived
in Caesarea. Cornelius was expecting them and had called
together his relatives and close friends. As Peter entered the

house, Cornelius met him and fell at his feet in reverence. But
Peter made him get up. 'Stand up', he said, 'I am only a man
myself.'

Talking with him, Peter went inside and found a large
gathering of people. He said to them, 'You are well aware that
it is against our law for a Jew to associate with a Gentile or visit
him. But God has shown me that I should not call any man
impure or unclean. So when I was sent for, I came without
raising any objection. May I ask why you sent for me?' (Acts:
10: 1–29)

Paul of Tarsus echoes Mark's comment when he says 'all
food is clean'. His mission to the Gentiles would have been
impossible if he had not been willing to consort with
Gentiles on equal terms, and he had cause to rebuke Peter
for failing to do so:

When Peter came to Antioch, I opposed him to his face,
because he was clearly in the wrong. Before certain men came
from James, he used to eat with the Gentiles. But when they
arrived, he began to draw back and separate himself from the
Gentiles because he was afraid of those who belonged to the
circumcision group. The other Jews joined him in his
hypocrisy, so that by their hypocrisy even Barnabas was led
astray.

When I saw that they were not acting in line with the truth of
the gospel, I said to Peter in front of them all, 'You are a Jew,
yet you live like a Gentile and not like a Jew. How is it, then,
that you force Gentiles to follow Jewish customs?' (Galatians
2: 11–14)

It is not to be supposed that the attitude of Jesus and His
apostles was something absolutely new in the life of Israel,
'the prophets rate ethical purity far above that which is
purely cultic. Hence the prophets prepare the way for the
religion of Jesus',[5] and the influence of the prophets is
clearly to be seen in the Psalms, one of which, Psalm 51,
scales heights of moral self-awareness scarcely achieved
elsewhere before the coming of Christ:

Have mercy on me, O God,
according to your unfailing love;
according to your great compassion
blot out my transgressions.
Wash away all my iniquity
and cleanse me from my sin.

For I know my transgressions,
and my sin is always before me.
Against you, you only, have I sinned
and done what is evil in your sight,
so that you are proved right when you speak
and justified when you judge.
Surely I was sinful at birth,
sinful from the time my mother conceived me.
Surely you desire truth in the inner parts;
you teach me wisdom in the inmost place.

Cleanse me with hyssop, and I shall be clean;
wash me, and I shall be whiter than snow.
Let me hear joy and gladness;
let the bones you have crushed rejoice.
Hide your face from my sins
and blot out all my iniquity.

Create in me a pure heart, O God,
and renew a steadfast spirit within me.
Do not cast me from your presence
or take your Holy Spirit from me.
Restore to me the joy of your salvation
and grant me a willing spirit, to sustain me.
(Psalm 51: 1-12)

It will be seen by now how the two phrases of the
Beatitude qualify and inform each other. Jesus set before
his disciples the Summon Bonum, the only worthwhile
objective for any human being, the vision of God. But He
clearly does not mean 'the flight of the alone to the alone'.
For Him, as a man, the Summum Bonum had been his
vivid and unfailing relationship with His heavenly

Father. When He was baptised He *saw* the Spirit of God descending like a dove and lighting on Him (Matthew 3: 16). When He went out into the wilderness He was conscious of being driven by the spirit (Mark 1: 12). When the seventy missioners returned with joy at their triumphs in the mission field Jesus said that He 'saw Satan fall like lightning from heaven' and at once He turned to His heavenly Father in prayer:

> At that time Jesus, full of joy through the Holy Spirit, said, 'I praise you, Father, Lord of heaven and earth, because you have hidden these things from the wise and learned, and revealed them to little children. Yes, Father, for this was your good pleasure.
>
> All things have been committed to me by my Father. No-one knows who the Son is except the Father, and no-one knows who the Father is except the Son and those to whom the Son chooses to reveal him.'
>
> Then he turned to his disciples and said privately, 'Blessed are the eyes that see what you see. For I tell you that many prophets and kings wanted to see what you see but did not see it, and to hear what you hear but did not hear it.' (Luke 10: 21-24)

But perhaps His own vision of God was never clearer or brighter than in the story of the Transfiguration:

> After six days Jesus took Peter, James and John with him and led them up a high mountain, where they were all alone. There he was transfigured before them. His clothes became dazzling white, whiter than anyone in the world could bleach them. And there appeared before them Elijah and Moses, who were talking with Jesus.
>
> Peter said to Jesus, 'Rabbi, it is good for us to be here. Let us put up three shelters – one for you, one for Moses and one for Elijah.' (He did not know what to say, they were so frightened.)
>
> Then a cloud appeared and enveloped them, and a voice came from the cloud:
>
> 'This is my Son, whom I love. Listen to him!'

Suddenly, when they looked round, they no longer saw anyone with them except Jesus. (Mark 9: 2–8)

So what He is offering to his disciples is no 'flight of the alone to the alone' or the arduous asceticisms of the Qumran community nor any sense of self-satisfaction based upon successful adherence to the Law, but an abiding sense of the presence of God similar to that which He enjoyed Himself, to be found in a single-minded devotion to God and His kingdom on earth within the circumstances, joyful and painful, of everyday life in Palestine or in Egypt, in New York or Singapore, on the factory floor and in the office block, in Milton Keynes and the North Oxfordshire village. 'No one has ever seen God, but God the One and Only, who is at the Father's side, has made him known' (John 1: 18). So at the end of his masterly book on *The Vision of God* as experienced in the course of history Dr. Kirk comes to this conclusion:

The doctrine that the 'end of man is the vision of God', as a practical maxim for life, implies that the Christian should set himself first of all to focus his thought upon God in the spirit of worship. It implies this of necessity, and of necessity it implies nothing more – nothing whatever as to the achieving of pleasures, rapture, exultation in the act of worship. The only achievement man has the right to hope for is that of greater Christian saintliness – greater zeal for service – coming from this direction of the heart and mind to God. It can hardly be denied that in so far as unselfishness is possible in this life at all (to anticipate for a moment another question) this is an unselfish deal. To look towards God, and from that 'look' to acquire insight both into the follies of one's own heart and the needs of one's neighbours, with power to correct the one no less than to serve the other – this is something very remote from any quest for 'religious experience' for its own sake. Yet this, and nothing else, is what the vision of God has meant in the fully developed thought of historic Christianity.[6]

It is, as Father Bremond suggests, 'one thing to learn

Baedeker by heart, to book your cabin on the next boat, to register your luggage, even to get half way up the gangplank; but in no language in the world does that make you a traveller.' Only the pure in heart will see God, those who, to use Kierkegaard's words, 'will one thing' – and travel.[7] They will not necessarily have dramatic experiences, they will not be spared tedious and frustrating circumstances in everyday life, they will not be enraptured or carried up into the seventh heaven but they will be travelling with One in whose face we actually see God.

*Chapter 11*

# BLESSED ARE THE PEACEMAKERS FOR THEY WILL BE CALLED SONS OF GOD

Judged by the number of sermons devoted to it in the *Expository Times*,[1] this Beatitude is seen to have an immediate relevance to our own society. In the midst of industrial unrest and international tension we cry out for peacemakers who will put the warmongers to flight and restore order to our streets, bring rationality to bear on some of our more intractable industrial disputes and, at a more personal level, create an atmosphere in which a husband and wife and parents and children can discover peace with each other. But what is it in fact that the preacher announcing his text is offering, and what is it that the congregation, settling down into their pews, are expecting? Are we to assume that conflict is always wrong and that the peacemaker is there to remove it?

It could be argued that all progress in almost any field of knowledge and in almost any walk of life is the product of conflict. The conquests of Alexander the Great in the fourth century B.C. created social and international chaos but they also released powers of mind and spirit which have influenced the Western world ever since. The history of the trade union movement in this country is the history of conflict, which may be regarded as out of place now but which, at the time, procured not only a living wage for the worker but a say in the democratic ordering of society. Churchmen still look back to a golden age, as they suppose it to be, when the Church was one and when men lived by a faith universally recognised, if not always honoured. Yet that so-called golden age was an age of deepening corruption and inner apostasy from which we were extricated by the Reformation. Every great institution occasionally needs a 'wild boar in its vineyard' if it is to remain vital and relevant. In the world of the intellect, in the world of the arts, in the world of science, the same holds true – the comfortable dogmas of a previous age come under threat and are drastically revised under the impact of conflict.

There are situations in which the peacemaker is neither welcome nor helpful – if his task is seen solely in terms of reducing the temperature and producing a compromise formula by which the warring parties may be reconciled. And there is one particular ideology dominant over a large part of the earth's surface where peacemakers are not welcome at all. Karl Marx, although in later life very critical of his mentor, was nevertheless deeply influenced by the teaching of Hegel, the great German idealist philosopher (1770–1831). I quote now a passage from Isaiah Berlin:[2]

> He [Hegel] insisted on the reality and necessity of conflicts and wars and revolutions, of the tragic waste and destruction in the world. He declared (following Fichte) that every process is one of necessary tension between incompatible forces, each straining against the other, and by this mutual conflict advancing their own development. This struggle is sometimes concealed and sometimes open, and can be traced in all provinces of conscious activity as the clash between so many rival physical, moral and intellectual attitudes and movements, each of which claims to provide total solutions and breeds new crises by its very one-sidedness; it grows in strength and sharpness until it turns into an open conflict which culminates in a final collision, the violence of which destroys

all the contenders. This is the point at which the hitherto continuous development is broken, a sudden leap takes place to a new level, whereupon the tension between a new cluster of forces begins once more. Certain among those leaps, those, namely, which occur on a sufficiently large and noticeable scale, are termed political revolutions. But, on a more trivial scale, they occur in every sphere of activity, in the arts and sciences, in the growth of physical organisms studied by biologists and in the atomic processes studied by chemists, and finally in ordinary argument between two opponents, when, in the conflict between two partial falsehoods, new truth is discovered, itself only relative, itself assaulted by a counter-truth, the destruction of each by the other leading once more to a new level in which the antagonistic elements are transfigured into a new organic whole – a process which continues without end . . .

The new methods of research and interpretation which had suddenly been revealed produced a startling, and even intoxicating, effect on enlightened German society, and to a lesser extent on its cultural dependencies, the Universities of St. Petersburg and Moscow. Hegelianism became the official creed of almost every man with intellectual pretensions.

So it is not as obvious as it might seem that peacemakers are blessed in a world where conflict is endemic and sometimes beneficial. We need therefore a deeper insight into the role of the peacemaker as Our Lord saw him before we can pronounce him 'blessed' or a 'Son of God'.

The word for 'peacemaker' in the text of this Beatitude occurs only once in the New Testament, although the verb occurs elsewhere at Colossians 1: 20. It means what it says – to make peace. Thus a successful Emperor can be called a 'peacemaker' if as a result of a victorious war he establishes peace in the world. Broadly speaking, in its earliest use in the secular world the word 'peace' is by way of being a negative concept to be understood in terms of absence of war – so rare a condition in the Ancient World as to deserve a special word. In the New Testament the word may be simply part of a greeting, e.g. 'go in peace', 'peace be unto you', 'the peace of God rule in your hearts', 'grace be unto you and peace', 'peace be to this house'. The word is particularly common in St. Luke's Gospel where it is used thirteen times and has a wide range of meanings. Zacharias spoke of the coming Messianic age when 'the dayspring from on high' would 'shine on those living in darkness and in the shadow of death, to guide our feet into the path of peace'. (Luke 1: 79) The message of the angel at the birth of Christ has a message of Glory to God in the highest and on earth peace among men of good will (Luke 2: 14). At the triumphal entry into Jerusalem the disciples began to rejoice and praise God with a loud voice saying, 'Blessed is the king who comes in the name of the Lord! Peace in heaven and glory in the highest!' (Luke 19: 38).

In St. John's Gospel, on the other hand, peace is seen less as a desirable social condition and more as an intensely personal experience:

Peace I leave with you; my peace I give you. I do not give to you as the world gives. Do not let your hearts be troubled and do not be afraid. (John 14: 27)

'I have told you these things, so that in me you may have peace. In this world you will have trouble. But take heart! I have overcome the world.' (John 16: 33)

On the evening of that first day of the week, when the disciples were together, with the doors locked for fear of the Jews, Jesus came and stood among them and said, 'Peace be with you!' (John 20: 19)

Peace within is by no means incompatible with conflict without; John says it is possible at the same time to experience tribulation in the world and peace in the heart. So the peacemaker is not exclusively concerned with removing the sources of conflict in society; if John is to be believed, the peacemaker has some responsibility for helping men and women to procure peace within. Indeed in a very striking passage Our Lord did not see Himself as a peacemaker in the former sense:

Do not suppose that I have come to bring peace to the earth. I did not come to bring peace, but a sword. For I have come to turn:
'a man against his father,
a daughter against her mother,
a daughter-in-law against her mother-in-law –
a man's enemies will be the members of his own household.'
(Matthew 10: 34–36)

If we assent to the conclusion that peace means more than a simple absence of war, then we shall have to go behind the Greek word of the New Testament to the Hebrew Word of the Old. It is a word which even the non-Hebraist will recognise. The visitor to Israel will hear Israelis saying it, singing it, though seldom it would seem enjoying it in a part of the world marked by incessant and bitter conflict. The word is *shalom*, a word so wide-ranging in its meaning that the Greek version of the Old Testament uses no fewer than twenty-three Greek words to express it. It was used in Old Testament times as it is used today as a form of greeting, and it certainly includes the meaning of absence of war. But in one place it stands for good health, in another for prosperity. The psalmist dreams of peace within the walls of Jerusalem and of the peace which comes from loving the Law of God. But it is Isaiah who reaches out towards the inner peace later to be enshrined in the fourth Gospel. I quote the words which have fallen like balm upon many a troubled soul and a fretful spirit – 'You will keep in perfect peace him whose mind is steadfast, because he trusts in you' (Isaiah 26: 3). It is the same prophet who reaches out towards a concept of peace expressed in social terms as well:

You women who are so complacent,
rise up and listen to me;
you daughters who feel secure,
hear what I have to say!
In little more than a year
you who feel secure will tremble;

the grape harvest will fail,
and the harvest of fruit will not come.
Tremble, you complacent women;
shudder, you daughters who feel secure!
Strip off your clothes,
put sackcloth round your waists,
Beat your breasts for the pleasant fields,
for the fruitful vines
and for the land of my people,
a land overgrown with thorns and briers –
yes, mourn for all houses of merriment
and for this city of revelry.
The fortress will be abandoned,
the noisy city deserted;
citadel and watchtower will become a wasteland for ever,
the delight of donkeys, a pasture for flocks,
till the Spirit is poured upon us from on high,
and the desert becomes a fertile field,
and the fertile field seems like a forest.
Justice will dwell in the desert
and righteousness live in the fertile field.
The fruit of righteousness will be peace;
the effect of righteousness will be quietness and confidence for
ever.
My people will live in peaceful dwelling-places,
in secure homes,
in undisturbed places of rest. (Isaiah 32: 9–18)

This is a particularly important passage because in it is
represented a whole range of meanings connected with
peace. The women of Jerusalem were, in one sense, at
peace, complacent, feeling secure. But that sense of
security was ill-founded and it was not very long before
they were putting sackcloth round their waists and
beating their breasts, when they were mourning for all
houses of merriment and for the city of revelry. But that
false peace, as Isaiah saw it, was ultimately to be replaced
by a true peace which is the fruit of righteousness. But that
true peace is not just to be an inner experience but
something which will inform social life as well – 'how

blessed you will be sowing your seed by every stream and letting your cattle and donkeys range free' (Isaiah 32: 20).

It is this same quality of peace which is envisaged in one of the most famous passages from Isaiah, famous because of its associations with the birth of Christ, inseparable in many people's minds from the haunting music of Handel's Messiah:

> The people walking in darkness
> have seen a great light;
> on those living in the land of the shadow of death
> a light has dawned.
> You have enlarged the nation
> and increased their joy;
> they rejoice before you
> as people rejoice at the harvest,
> as men rejoice
> when dividing the plunder.
> For as in the day of Midian's defeat,
> you have shattered
> the yoke that burdens them,
> the bar across their shoulders,
> the rod of their oppressor.
> Every warrior's boot used in battle
> and every garment rolled in blood
> will be destined for burning,
> will be fuel for the fire.
> For to us a child is born,
> to us a son is given,
> and the government will be on his shoulders.
> And he will be called
> Wonderful Counsellor, Mighty God
> Everlasting Father, Prince of Peace.
> Of the increase of his government and peace
> there will be no end.
> He will reign on David's throne
> and over his kingdom,
> establishing and upholding it
> with justice and righteousness
> from that time on and for ever.

The zeal of the Lord Almighty
will accomplish this. (Isaiah 9: 2-7)

It was this kind of peace which became associated in the tradition of the Church forever with the ultimate rule of Christ over all the earth – peace which is more than absence of war, more than prosperity and good health, more even than that inner peace which passes all understanding. Christ was to be a peacemaker not in the sense that he was to establish peace on the basis of successful conquest like the Roman emperor, He was to be a peacemaker in that He was to establish and uphold a kingdom in justice and righteousness. If Isaiah was not alone in this vision of the coming of peace, *shalom* achieved its richest and profoundest meaning through the glowing colours with which he painted it. It was to be an 'everlasting peace attended by an inconceivable harmony extending throughout the entire cosmos, and man will make that state of bliss completely his own, for the disease of sin will be fully healed in him.'[3]

It is with this rather enlarged view of peace that we move now to a consideration of the second half of the Beatitude where it is said that peacemakers will be called 'sons of God'. So far we have been content to speak of peace in general terms which would apply equally to civilisations and cultures as various as Babylon, Athens, Rome, Berlin, Paris, London or Leeds. Peace is what we aspire to if we do little enough to make it. But the Beatitude was first uttered in the first half of the first century, some forty years before the fall of Jerusalem. The Jews then as now prayed diligently for the peace of Jerusalem. They had good cause to, because Israel itself was bitterly divided by warring factions, less concerned to make peace than to establish a stockade from which to hurl bitter epithets and shoot sharp arrows at their enemies. It was one of the practical problems for Jesus of Nazareth that He was forever being associated in the public mind with one or other of these factions. The Pharisees would have been glad to claim Him for their own as a man committed to the renewal of Israel as they saw it. The Sadducees would have valued His support in their ceaseless conflict with the Pharisees. The followers of John the Baptist were incensed when they saw that He was making more disciples than their own master. The Zealots, those violent exponents of revolution, would eagerly have enrolled Him in their cause – and no doubt Herod would have been glad of His political support or at least acquiescence. There were many warmongers and few peacemakers, and it was when Jesus looked out on this scene of confusion and strife that He spoke with feeling to His nearest disciples of the blessedness of the peacemakers.

It was not to be. It was at least as much due to the internal feuding in Israel as to Roman imperial ambitions that the city of peace was ultimately besieged and totally destroyed. It was no doubt something like this that Our Lord had in mind when He wept over the city and said:

> If you, even you, had only known on this day what would bring you peace – but now it is hidden from your eyes. The days will come upon you when your enemies will build an embankment against you and encircle you and hem you in on every side. They will dash you to the ground, you and the children within your walls. They will not leave one stone on another because you did not recognise the time of God's coming to you. (Luke 19: 42–44)

It may be presumed, therefore, that if the first half of the Beatitude had a specific reference in the circumstances of Our Lord's own day it is likely that the second half of the Beatitude similarly had a specific reference. What did He mean when He said that the peacemakers would be called sons of God? The term 'Son of God' in the singular is commonly though not exclusively associated with Jesus Himself. The term 'sons of God' in the plural is relatively rare in the English translation, but that is misleading to the casual reader, because the term used in the Beatitude is elsewhere translated 'children of God'. So, Luke says of those who love their enemies that they should be 'children of the Highest' (Luke 6: 35, A.V.). St. Paul speaks of those who are led by the spirit of God as being sons (or children) of God. He speaks of those who are sons (or children) of God through faith in Christ (Galatians 3: 26). He explains that we are sons (children) because God sent forth the spirit of His son into our hearts crying *'Abba,* Father' (Galatians 4: 6). It is this double usage in the English translation which is confusing and makes the Beatitude all that more difficult to understand.

So let us ask what the phrase 'sons of God' would have meant to those who first heard it used in association with the blessing of peacemakers. On the whole the relationship between the God of Israel and the people of Israel was a relationship conceived in terms of master and servant, lord and slave, king and subject, but in some branches of later Judaism the relationship began to be conceived not in terms of lord and slave or master and servant but in terms of father and son. Prayers begin to be offered to God as father (Ecclesiasticus 23: 1) and the observant Jew, loyal to the Law, may be accounted a 'son of God' (Wisdom 2: 13). It is not entirely without precedent in the older literature. See for example Hosea 1: 10. 'In the place where it was said to them, "You are not my people", they will be called "sons of the living God".' The term 'sons of God' would therefore have had a certain resonance in the minds of those of Our Lord's hearers who were familiar with their Jewish heritage, in so far as it suggested another category of those who might be called 'the sons of God', i.e. not just the loyal members of Israel or the observers of the Law, but of those who, of whatever race or religion, were peacemakers.

I apologise for the semantic complexities of the previous paragraph. They arise out of the inevitable limitations within which any translator has to work. To convey the meaning of the original language he may employ as many as nine or ten words in different contexts for one word in the original. On the other hand, for the same reason, he may use the same word in English to translate nine or ten different words in the original language. It is this factor which makes it peculiarly difficult for the English reader to interpret this Beatitude. So may I try to illuminate the Beatitude by way of suppositions. We know that one Roman Emperor, Commodus, took to himself the title of 'peacemaker'. But that was over a hundred years later than the period in which the New Testament was written. Let us suppose, however (and I know no evidence for it), that the Emperor Tiberius, of Our Lord's own day, had taken to himself that title. In that case Our Lord would have been saying – 'the real peacemakers are not those who impose peace by means of successful conquest or by political skills, but those who make peace possible by their attitude to life, by their humility of mind and openness of spirit.' And now to the second supposition. Suppose that there had been a sect current in Our Lord's lifetime which prided itself on its exclusive relationship with God and called its members 'sons of God'. There is some evidence for this in so far as the literature of the Qumran sect includes references to Psalm 2: 7, 'The Lord said to me you are My son, this day have I begotten you,' and applies the Psalm to the members of the sect. In that case Our Lord would be saying – 'It is not those who call themselves "sons of God" who are His sons but those who make peace across the barricades that divide Jew from Jew, Jew from Gentile, Jew from Samaritan.' That would have been in keeping with Our Lord's general attitude to the divisions in Israel and would certainly give the Beatitude a particular point. Even to engage in such speculation does help to deliver us from the notion that Our Lord spoke in vague generalities. Like every effective minister of the Gospel His message was to the men, women and children in front of Him in their particular personal, social and political concerns, long before it became a message to all mankind bound up in black covers and delivered with a sonorous voice in some splendid edifice of Christendom to a congregation two thousand years distant from the actual Sermon on the real Mount.

Even without the benefit of supposition the Beatitude certainly seems to suggest a disavowal of the exclusive privileges of Jewry. Once it is established that it is not just Jewish peacemakers who can be called 'sons of God', it follows that men of other races and religions may be called 'sons of God'. This is, in fact, exactly the stance adopted by St. Paul. His controversy with the other apostles arose from their initial insistence that non-Jewish believers should be circumcised. Paul's point was that men did not have to become Jews in order to become 'sons of God'; they were 'sons of God' by virtue of their faith in Christ. The argument is expressed in its boldest and most radical form in his letter to the Galatians (Galatians 4: 4-7).

> But when the time had fully come, God sent his Son, born of a woman, born under law, to redeem those under law, that we might receive the full rights of sons. Because you are sons, God sent the Spirit of his Son into our hearts, the Spirit who calls out, '*Abba*, Father.' So you are no longer a slave, but a son; and since you are a son, God has made you also an heir.

The argument appears again in his magisterial treatment of the problem in Romans 8: 12-17.

> Therefore, brothers, we have an obligation – but it is not to the sinful nature, to live according to it. For if you live according to the sinful nature, you will die; but if by the Spirit you put to death the misdeeds of the body, you will live, because those who are led by the Spirit of God are sons of God. For you did not receive a spirit that makes you a slave again to fear, but you received the Spirit of sonship. And by him we cry, '*Abba*, Father'. The Spirit himself testifies with our spirit that we are God's children. Now if we are children, then we are heirs –

heirs of God and co-heirs with Christ, if indeed we share in his sufferings in order that we may also share in his glory.

St. Paul did not have the Gospels in the form known to us in front of him, neither did he show much familiarity with the actual words of Christ, but his argument flows naturally from what we know of Our Lord's words and deeds. In the Sermon on the Mount itself He is recorded as saying:

> You have heard that it was said, 'Love your neighbour and hate your enemy.' But I tell you, Love your enemies and pray for those who persecute you, that you may be sons of your Father in heaven. He causes his sun to rise on the evil and the good, and sends rain on the righteous and the unrighteous. If you love those who love you, what reward will you get? Are not even the tax collectors doing that? And if you greet only your brothers, what are you doing more than others? Do not even pagans do that? Be perfect, therefore, as your heavenly Father is perfect. (Matthew 5: 43–48)

God causes His sun to rise on the Jew and the Gentile, and sends rain on the Pharisees and the Sadducees, the Herodians and the Zealots, the Essenes and the followers of John the Baptist; they are all capable of becoming 'sons of God'. But His deeds spoke louder than His words; He crossed the barriers as a peacemaker when He sat at the well with the Samaritan woman and healed the daughter of a Syro-phoenician; when He kept table company with sinners and healed a Roman centurion's servant. It was in fact the essence of His message. God was not just the God of the Jews but of all mankind, and sonship of God was available to all who put their trust in Him.

This teaching is carried to its logical and most powerful conclusion in the fourth Gospel:

> To the Jews who had believed him, Jesus said, 'If you hold to my teaching, you are really my disciples. Then you will know

the truth, and the truth will set you free.'

They answered him, 'We are Abraham's descendants and have never been slaves of anyone. How can you say that we shall be set free?'

Jesus replied, 'I tell you the truth, everyone who sins is a slave to sin. Now a slave has no permanent place in the family, but a son belongs to it for ever. So if the Son sets you free, you will be free indeed. I know you are Abraham's descendants. Yet you are ready to kill me, becase you have no room for my word. I am telling you what I have seen in the Father's presence, and you do what you have heard from your father.'

'Abraham is our father,' they answered.

'If you were Abraham's children,' said Jesus, 'then you would do the things Abraham did. As it is, you are determined to kill me, a man who has told you the truth that I heard from God. Abraham did not do such things. You are doing the things your own father does.'

'We are not illegitimate children,' they protested. 'The only Father we have is God himself.'

Jesus said to them, 'If God were your Father, you would love me, for I come from God and now am here. I have not come on my own; but he sent me.' (John 8: 31-42)

This passage will repay careful consideration. It arises out of a controversy between Jesus and the Jewish leaders of His day, a controversy which unhappily sharpened and deepened in the subsequent life of the Church. Nevertheless, many an abiding truth has arisen out of what we might call 'unfortunate' controversy and the abiding truth is here expressed with rare force. The implications of the passage are that there was indeed something special about Jesus' relationship with the God of Abraham, Isaac and Jacob. He was not only a prophet, or only a teacher, or only a healer; He enjoyed an experience of God which could only be expressed in terms of the intimacy between a father and his only son. That is why He never uses the phrase 'our Father' in such a way as to suggest that His disciples enjoyed that same relationship. 'I am ascending to my Father and your Father, to my God and your God'

(John 20: 17, R.V.) was as far as He could go. The second implication is that a way was being opened by which those same disciples could enjoy, although at a different level, the experience of sonship. They too would learn to call on God as '*Abba*, Father'; they too, to use St. Paul's expression, would be 'sons of God'. The distinction between Jesus and His disciples in this regard is well made by Josef Blinzler;[4]

> The uniqueness of the sonship of Jesus Christ appears in the Johannine writings in the fact that he has a special terminology for it, the title 'son of God' being reserved for Christ alone. In so far as John speaks of men being sons of God at all, he never employs the term 'sons' but invariably confines himself to the phrase 'children of God' to express this. This derivative childhood of God is for him, just as for Paul, a blessing of salvation which has already been imparted in the present life to those who believe in his name, that is in Jesus as Messiah and Son of God.

I have attempted to expound the meaning of the two phrases – 'the peacemakers' and 'the sons of God', but it now remains to draw the two halves of the Beatitude together and show how they relate to each other. The will of God is peace for all mankind, not simply in terms of absence of war but in terms of richer personal relationships lived out at the family, national and international level. He wills that all mankind shall be a 'Jerusalem', a city of peace in which the ruler shall be known as Melchizedek, king of righteousness and king of peace (Hebrews 7: 1-3). Philo, the Jewish philosopher of Alexandria, goes so far as to describe God Himself as 'peacemaker'. It follows that those who are called of God to be His servants are under obligation likewise to exhibit His nature and to become peacemakers. This is not to be understood in terms of being willing to undertake delicate reconciliations or to provide formulas for the settlement of an industrial dispute or indeed to play such a part in the chancelleries of Europe (although that role is certainly not excluded). It does mean that the man who enjoys an intimate relationship with God as a son with a father should be prepared to face the pain and distress which is inseparable from life lived on the frontier between warring armies or warring classes. It could hardly be better put than by Dietrich Bonhoeffer:[5]

> The followers of Jesus have been called to peace. When he called them they found their peace, for he is their peace. But now they are told that they must not only *have* peace but *make* it. And to that end they renounce all violence and tumult. In the cause of Christ nothing is to be gained by such methods. His kingdom is one of peace, and the mutual greeting of his flock is a greeting of peace. His disciples keep the peace by choosing to endure suffering themselves rather than inflict it on others. They maintain fellowship where others would break it off. They renounce all self-assertion, and quietly suffer in the face of hatred and wrong. In so doing they overcome evil with good, and establish the peace of God in the midst of a world of war and hate. But nowhere will that peace be more manifest than where they meet the wicked in peace and are ready to suffer at their hands. The peacemakers will carry the cross with their Lord, for it was on the cross that peace was made. Now that they are partners in Christ's work of reconciliation, they are called the sons of God as he is the Son of God.

I have suggested that peacemakers ought not to feel excluded from participation in the day-to-day peace-making that needs to be done at a personal level and in social and international relationships. There is everything to be said for 'sons of God' who are prepared to give their minds and their hearts to the unravelling of the disputes which so disfigure our society and destroy our hopes of *shalom*. By way of illustration, therefore, I end this chapter with two quotations which contrast vividly with each other, not only in their underlying assumption but in their method of approach. The first is a record of an interview with Arthur Scargill in the New Left Review, reproduced in *The Times* under the headline 'My Greatest Day'. It was a long interview but the following extracts give the flavour:

> Then we launched pickets into Nottinghamshire and Derbyshire. We decided that the best way that we could produce an effective stoppage was to have a rapid mobile picket. We'd used this before in the Yorkshire coalfield, but on a very limited scale and *never* in an organised way. We launched from the coalfield here squads of cars, minibuses and buses, all directed onto predetermined targets, with five, six, seven hundred miners at a time. Of course, the police were going to come, but they couldn't cover forty points at a time, without bringing the British armed forces in.
>
> I believe in a class war you have to fight with the tools at your disposal. 1969 was a foretaste... a number of us had launched an organisation called the Barnsley Miners' Forum, of which I was secretary. This forum was a platform for the left and a platform for ideas within the movement... We left a token picket at the docks, moved on, and closed down the power stations one by one. Within two days we'd shut down the whole of East Anglia... out to defeat Heath and Heath's policies because we were fighting a government. Anyone who thinks otherwise was living in cloud-cuckoo land. We had to declare *war* on them and the only way you could declare war was to attack the vulnerable points... the miners' union was not opposed to the distribution of coal. We were only opposed to the distribution of coal to industry because we wished to paralyse the nation's economy. It's as simple as that. We were fighting a class war and you don't fight a war with sticks and bladders. You fight a war with the weapons that are going to win it...
>
> The solidarity of the working class was never more evident. On that Thursday it produced the greatest day of my life... I gave a political speech to that mass of people and told them that it was the greatest victory of the working class, certainly in my lifetime...
>
> You know the words: 'Unity is Strength', 'Workers of the

World Unite', 'Man to Man Brother Be'. They're big words. Sometimes they'd been ridiculed. Through all that ridicule, all that sneering, they survived. Here was the living proof that the working class had only to flex its muscles and it could bring governments, employers, society to a total standstill . . .

The second illustration is from a book by Paul Petrocokino *The Heart of it All*:[6]

A Japanese woman senator, a socialist, formerly a Marxist, had found the beginning of a faith in God. She had found a new relationship with her husband and their home had been remade. Her party was in opposition when she learnt that the Government was planning to send a trade mission to many of the Pacific nations with which Japan had been at war and which had suffered at the hands of the Japanese. She had a compelling thought, which she believed came from the mind of God, to go and see the Prime Minister and tell him that the need was for Japan humbly to ask forgiveness of each nation she had wronged, and that without such an apology the mission would fail hopelessly. With much trepidation she called on the Prime Minister and found him meeting with some of his Cabinet. She told him the thought she had had. His face gave no clue as to how he reacted. Wherever he went, however, including some countries that planned to give him a hostile reception, Prime Minister Kishi first asked forgiveness for what his nation had done and spoke too of practical steps of reparation that Japan would make. This mission was described as 'the statesmanship of the humble heart'. It helped beyond all measure to create new relationships in the Pacific.

The first illustration describes a highly sophisticated political exercise based on sound Marxist dogma which glorifies conflict as the way to the society of our dreams. Peacemakers are not necessary and will not be welcome. The second illustration is a simple, artless account of how one woman, herself formerly a Marxist, took seriously her role as a child of God and as a peacemaker and in so doing created a new atmosphere of trust and hope. Broadly speaking, the world is divided between those who do or do not live on the basis of this Beatitude - Blessed are the peacemakers, they shall be called sons of God.

*Chapter 12*

# BLESSED ARE THOSE WHO HAVE BEEN PERSECUTED FOR RIGHTEOUSNESS' SAKE FOR THEIRS IS THE KINGDOM OF HEAVEN

The meaning of this Beatitude is complicated by the existence of another version of it (so it would seem) in St. Luke's Gospel:

> Blessed are you when men hate you,
> when they exclude you and insult you
> and reject your name as evil,
> because of the Son of Man. (Luke 6: 22)

St. Matthew's version at this point seems to look backwards to those who 'have been persecuted'. St. Luke's version looks unambiguously forward to those who will be hated, excluded and insulted.

As, verbally, the two versions bear little relationship to each other the obvious solution is that the two evangelists had access to different sources. We have no means of knowing which was the original just as we have no grounds for preferring, in general, Matthew's or Luke's treatment of the Sermon as a whole. St. Luke's version of this Beatitude has all the appearance of vividness and

originality and if it was the original it is difficult to see
how it could have achieved the Matthaean form. On the
other hand, if Matthew is the original it is difficult to see
how in the chemistry of Luke's mind it achieved such
vividness of utterance. It could be said that Luke in his
companionship with St. Paul on his missionary journeys
was well acquainted with being 'hated, excluded, rejected'.
Matthew, though well acquainted with the tensions that
would ultimately issue in persecution, may not actually
have experienced them himself. But in the end we are
going to have to say that there is no wholly convincing
explanation of the variation between the two versions;
neither does the one version helpfully inform the other. So
I shall have to treat St. Matthew's version in its own right
without looking for much assistance from St. Luke and I
shall have to treat it as an original utterance of Christ
without regard to the claims that could be made for the
originality of Luke.

However, the contrast between them does highlight the
fact that at this particular point Matthew appears to have
in mind not just the sufferings of the first disciples or of
their descendants, but the sufferings of the past, lavishly
illustrated for example in the roll-call of the Epistle to the
Hebrews:

> Others were tortured and refused to be released, so that they
> might gain a better resurrection. Some faced jeers and
> flogging, while still others were chained and put in prison.
> They were stoned, they were sawn in two; they were put to
> death by the sword. They went about in sheepskins and
> goatskins, destitute, persecuted and ill-treated – the world was
> not worthy of them. They wandered in deserts and mountains,
> and in caves and holes in the ground.
>     These were all commended for their faith, yet none of them
> received what had been promised. God had planned some-
> thing better for us so that only together with us would they be
> made perfect. (Hebrews 11: 35–40)

The root meaning of the Hebrew word normally

though not invariably translated 'persecute' is to pursue, to hunt down, and it is a measure of the frequency of this experience in the history of Israel that the word occurs one hundred and thirty times in the Hebrew Bible. But, in addition, there are many instances where the experience is described either by the use of another word or is implied by the context. Cain for example persecuted Abel (Genesis 4), and why? 'Because his own actions were evil and his brother's were righteous' (1 John 3: 12). Esau (although with better cause) persecuted Jacob. Joseph's brothers persecuted Joseph and sold him into Egypt. King Saul for much the same reasons, I suppose, as Cain persecuted Abel, persecuted David. But the classic instance of persecution for religious as distinct from personal reasons is the story contained in 1 Kings 18. Elijah began it by confronting the prophets of Baal on Mount Carmel in a contest of power which culminated in the defeat and slaughter of the prophets of Baal. Jezebel, herself a patron of Baal, responded with similar ferocity to Elijah, '"May the gods deal with me, be it ever so severely, if by this time tomorrow I do not make your life like that of one of them." Elijah was afraid and ran for his life' (1 Kings 19: 2–3).

In the post-exilic period, after the collapse of Israel as a nation-state, references to persecution become more plentiful and more stereotyped. The psalmists frequently refer to it as a contemporary fact of life and it is particularly prominent in what we might otherwise think an unusual context – in Psalm 119, a psalm which expresses the author's arduous and costly devotion to the Law. 'When will you punish my persecutors?' he asks (verse 84); 'men persecute me without cause' (verse 86 and verse 161); 'they draw near who persecute me with evil purpose, they are far from your Law' (verse 150, R.S.V.); 'many are my persecutors and my adversaries but I do not swerve from your testimonies' (verse 157, R.S.V.). There are many more references to persecution in this particular psalm but these are sufficient to show the intimate connection in the author's mind between persecution and the Law. By his time in the post-exilic period the Jewish people are a scattered race, many of them living in the ghettos of the Ancient World, clinging to their ancestral faith, making themselves conspicuous by their devotion to ritual and dietary regulations and inevitably exposing themselves to the kind of savageries which we associate with anti-Semitism then as now.

The Book of Daniel addresses itself to a similar situation at much the same time:

It pleased Darius to appoint 120 satraps to rule throughout the kingdom, with three administrators over them, one of whom was Daniel. The satraps were made accountable to them so that the king might not suffer loss. Now Daniel so distinguished himself among the administrators and the satraps by his exceptional qualities that the king planned to set him over the whole kingdom. At this, the administrators and the satraps tried to find grounds for charges against Daniel in his conduct of government affairs, but they were unable to do so. They could find no corruption in him, because he was trustworthy and neither corrupt nor negligent. Finally these men said, 'We will never find any basis for charges against this man Daniel unless it has something to do with the law of his God.'

So the administrators and the satraps went as a group to the king and said, 'O King Darius, live for ever! The royal administrators, prefects, satraps, advisers and governors have all agreed that the king should issue an edict and enforce the decree that anyone who prays to any god or man during the next thirty days, except to you, O king, shall be thrown into the lions' den. Now, O king, issue the decree and put it in writing . . .'

Now when Daniel learned that the decree had been published, he went home to his upstairs room where the windows opened towards Jerusalem. Three times a day he got down on his knees and prayed, giving thanks to his God, just as he had done before. Then these men went as a group and found Daniel praying and asking God for help. So they went to the king and spoke to him about his royal decree. 'Did you not publish a decree that during the next thirty days anyone who prays to any god or man except to you, O king, would be thrown into the lions' den?'

The king answered, 'The decree stands – in accordance with the laws of the Medes and Persians, which cannot be repealed.'

Then they said to the king, 'Daniel, who is one of the exiles from Judah, pays no attention to you, O king, or to the decree you put in writing. He still prays three times a day.' When the king heard this, he was greatly distressed; he was determined to rescue Daniel and made every effort until sundown to save him.

Then the men went as a group to the king and said to him, 'Remember, O king, that according to the law of the Medes and Persians no decree or edict that the king issues can be changed.'

So the king gave the order, and they brought Daniel and threw him into the lions' den. The king said to Daniel, 'May your God, whom you serve continually, rescue you!' (Daniel 6: 1–16)

This is persecution of the most blatant kind, arising no doubt out of jealousy of Daniel's position but fuelled by a hatred of the genuine, if ostentatious, religious practice of a minority group.

Persecution was not confined to the persecution of Israel by a foreign power. It arose also out of bitter divisions within Israel itself whereby the religious establishment persecuted those who, for whatever reason, resisted it in the name of the Law of God. Jeremiah, for example, did not suffer persecution by the enemies of his race but by those of his own faith. 'Remember me and care for me. Avenge me on my persecutors' he said (Jeremiah 15: 15). 'Let my persecutors be put to shame, but keep me from shame; let them be terrified, but keep me from terror' (Jeremiah 17: 18). 'The Lord is with me like a mighty warrior, so my persecutors will stumble and not prevail' (Jeremiah 20: 11). A similar situation is described in the Wisdom of Solomon dating from the first or second century B.C.:

Come on therefore, let us enjoy the good things that are

present; and let us speedily use the creatures like as in youth.

Let us fill ourselves with costly wine and ointments; and let no flower of the spring pass by us:

Let us crown ourselves with rosebuds, before they be withered:

Let none of us go without his part of our voluptuousness: let us leave tokens of our joyfulness in every place: for this is our portion, and our lot is this.

Let us oppress the poor righteous man, let us not spare the widow, nor reverence the ancient gray hairs of the aged.

Let our strength be the law of justice: for that which is feeble is found to be nothing worth.

Therefore let us lie in wait for the righteous; because he is not for our turn, and he is clean contrary to our doings: he upbraideth us with our offending the law, and objecteth to our infamy the transgressings of our education.

He professeth to have the knowledge of God: and he calleth himself the child of the Lord.

He was made to reprove our thoughts.

He is grievous unto us even to behold: for his life is not like other men's, his ways are of another fashion.

We are esteemed of him as counterfeits: he abstaineth from our ways as from filthiness: he pronounceth the end of the just to be blessed, and maketh his boast that God is his father.

Let us see if his words be true: and let us prove what shall happen in the end of him.

For if the just man be the son of God, he will help him, and deliver him from the hand of his enemies.

Let us examine him with despitefulness and torture, that we may know his meekness, and prove his patience.

Let us condemn him with a shameful death: for by his own saying he shall be respected. (Wisdom of Solomon 2: 6-20)

It is not too difficult therefore to see the source of Matthew's version of this Beatitude. Illustrations of persecution were readily to hand from the sacred Scriptures. Contemporary history would have provided him with similar illustrations, for the period before the birth of Christ was marked by fierce enmity between those who wished to take advantage of the cultural and political opportunities of the Greek world and those who resolutely resisted them in the name of true religion and the unchanging Law of God. Persecution was bitten into the heart and mind of men, possibly like Matthew himself, who had suffered for their devotion to the Law in a society largely alienated from it.[1] The historical experience of persecution, so persistent and so ubiquitous, does call for explanation, much as anti-Semitism in our own time calls for explanation, and it is to this explanation that we now turn.

If this were a sermon and I were looking for a text I could turn to St. Paul who, every bit as much as Jeremiah, or Daniel, suffered persecution for righteousness' sake:

> Now you, brothers, like Isaac, are children of promise. At that time the son born in the ordinary way persecuted the son born by the power of the Spirit. It is the same now. (Galatians 4: 28-29)

But whilst that text is a useful marker it does not in itself do justice to the range of interpretative principles embedded in the life and literature of Israel. The question is, why do the righteous suffer for righteousness' sake when, as they believe, they are engaged on the Lord's business? Why does not God swiftly vindicate the godly, descending from heaven to frustrate and scatter their enemies?

We are not immune to that question ourselves in the twentieth century. The Holocaust Museum in Israel is a grisly reminder of the tragedies that have overtaken that nation – but not only that nation. World history is full of examples of those who have suffered for righteousness' sake. Can it be said that they are blessed – the Armenians, for example, or the Quakers, or the Waldensians, or the victims of the Inquisition, or the recusant priests? The Jews were amongst the first but certainly not the last to ask the question of the martyrs under the altar in the Book of

Revelations – 'How long, Sovereign Lord, holy and true, until you judge the inhabitants of the earth and avenge our blood?' (Revelation 6: 10)

There are several explanations hinted at within the pages of sacred Scripture. The wise man of Ecclesiasticus, looking back over his own life and the life of his people, has this to say on the subject:

> My son, if thou come to serve the Lord, prepare thy soul for temptation.
>
> Set thy heart aright, and constantly endure, and make not haste in time of trouble.
>
> Cleave unto him, and depart not away, that thou mayest be increased at thy last end.
>
> Whatsoever is brought upon thee take cheerfully, and be patient when thou art changed to a low estate.
>
> For gold is tried in the fire, and acceptable men in the furnace of adversity.
>
> Believe in him, and he will help thee; order thy way aright, and trust in him.
>
> Ye that fear the Lord, wait for his mercy; and go not aside, lest ye fall.
>
> Ye that fear the Lord, believe him; and your reward shall not fail.
>
> Ye that fear the Lord, hope for good, and for everlasting joy and mercy.
>
> Look at the generations of old, and see; did ever any trust in the Lord, and was confounded? or did any abide in his fear, and was forsaken? or whom did he ever despise, that called upon him?
>
> For the Lord is full of compassion and mercy, long-suffering and very pitiful, and forgiveth sins, and saveth in time of affliction. (Ecclesiasticus 2: 1–11)

So, persecution is one of the aspects of life which makes men aware of their need of God and encourages them to 'fall into the hands of the Lord . . . for as his majesty is so also is his mercy' (Ecclesiasticus 2: 18).

For more robust souls (and the prophets were amongst

them) persecution was more than the common lot of all humanity; it was God's instrument for creating a purified people, tested in the fires of affliction, who would one day inherit the kingdom prepared from the foundation of the world; they would shine as stars in the firmament, would be a light to lighten the Gentiles, would be the agents for a renewed earth and a renewed heaven. 'Heady talk', you may say, fit for the pulpit, but hardly for the arena or the gallows or the prison cell. Nevertheless, it sustained heroic souls in Israel for generation after generation.

The most profound explanation is that suggested by the unknown prophet of Isaiah 53. Having described in typical 'persecution language' the fate of the unknown prophet, the author offers this astonishing explanation of it:

Yet it was the Lord's will to crush him and cause him to suffer,
and though the Lord makes his life a guilt offering,
he will see his offspring and prolong his days,
and the will of the Lord will prosper in his hand.
After the suffering of his soul,
he will see the light of life and be satisfied,
by his knowledge my righteous servant will justify many,
and he will bear their iniquities.
Therefore I will give him a portion among the great,
and he will divide the spoils with the strong,
because he poured out his life unto death,
and was numbered with the transgressors.
For he bore the sin of many,
and made intercession for the transgressors. (Isaiah 53: 10–12)

This is a view of life wrought out in the deepest places of a man's heart as he tries to come to terms with the long, grim story of Israel's persecution. This passage has in New Testament times come to be applied to Christ, and it is indeed a potent commentary on His life and death. But originally it could have been intended as a comment on the life and sufferings of Israel itself, described here under the figure 'the servant of God'. It was a bold and uncompromising utterance – persecution is not to be regretted, resisted or even explained; it is to be accepted as part of the vocation of the chosen people, chosen not for power or influence in the world but for submission to it for the glory of God. This is a hard saying, who can bear it? The answer is that nobody could bear it until Jesus of Nazareth saw in this passage from Isaiah 53 a profile of His own life and death.

Jesus of Nazareth had His own moments of success, popular acclaim and spiritual exaltation. Yet from a relatively early period within His ministry the blue sky was occasionally and increasingly darkened by the thought of His own vocation; He was to be the lonely representative of the chosen people bearing in His own mind and body the burden of the world's salvation. He was, like the prophets before Him, to be persecuted by the religious establishment of His day but in that persecution, freely and devotedly accepted, He was to be the light of the Gentiles which His own people had failed to be.

He took up our infirmities and carried our sorrow . . . He was pierced for our transgressions, He was crushed for our iniquities . . . He was oppressed and afflicted . . . He was assigned a grave with the wicked and with the rich in His death, though He had done no violence nor was any deceit in His mouth. (Isaiah 53: 4,5,7,9)

Blessed is he who has been persecuted – 'He shall see the result of the suffering of his soul and be satisfied' (Isaiah 53: 11).

It is hardly surprising, if this is indeed the import of Our Lord's life and work, that the language of persecution is as prominent in the New Testament as in the Old. It receives its most comprehensive treatment in St. Paul's Second Letter to the Corinthians which abounds with the language of persecution. For example:

But we have this treasure in jars of clay to show that this all-surpassing power is from God and not from us. We are hard pressed on every side, but not crushed; perplexed, but not in despair; persecuted, but not abandoned; struck down, but not destroyed. We always carry around in our body the death of Jesus, so that the life of Jesus may also be revealed in our body. For we who are alive are always being given over to death for Jesus' sake, so that his life may be revealed in our mortal body. So then, death is at work in us, but life is at work in you. (2 Corinthians 4: 7–12)

Thus, on the basis of the New Testament Dr. Selwyn is able to speak about a 'philosophy of persecution'.[2] This philosophy compares and contrasts with the attitudes of the Jewish people to their experience of persecution. The apocalyptic tradition in Israel had envisaged the end of the world in terms of signs in heaven and earth, cosmic warfare, the rise and fall of earthly kingdoms. These expectations play a part in the New Testament apocalyptic as well. But, as Dr. Selwyn says, persecution for the faith was part of a distinctively Christian view of the end of the world; it represents a definite addition to the features of the Jewish eschatalogical expectation and one that profoundly modified its spirit and structure.[3] The Jewish people had seen their experience of persecution and suffering as probationary, that is, a means by which the nation and individuals within it were to be brought to a peak of moral and spiritual excellence. In the Christian 'philosophy of persecution' this is expressed in dynamic terms, for example, in Acts 14: 22 where Paul is said to have returned to Antioch 'strengthening the disciples and encouraging them to remain true to the faith.' 'We must go through many hardships to enter the kingdom of God,' he said. Prominent amongst the 'hardships' was undoubtedly the experience of persecution both by Jews and Gentiles. In this saying, as Dr. Selwyn rightly says, the apostles crystallised their belief about persecution into dogmatic form. But St. Paul dared to go even further.

One of the proof texts current in the early Church was the one previously quoted from Isaiah 53, in which the death of Christ was seen in sacrifical terms as on behalf of all mankind 'wounded for our transgressions, bruised for our iniquities.' Something of the same 'philosophy of persecution' is to be found, however dimly, in St. Paul's own writing. In the passage previously quoted from 2 Corinthians 4: 12 he says 'death works in us but life in you.' There is what Charles Williams once called a kind of exchange in which the faithful acceptance of suffering somehow avails for the liberation and forgiveness of others. In Colossians 1: 24 Paul even dares to say, 'Now I rejoice in what was suffered for you, and I fill up in my flesh what is still lacking in regard to Christ's afflictions, for the sake of His body, which is the church.' These are bold words, open to much misunderstanding, but they are certainly part of a Christian philosophy of persecution. Blessed are those in this sense at least who have been persecuted for righteousness' sake.

This view of blessedness, so alien to the natural man in us all, so contrary to the world's view of happiness, has received powerful support from a recent book by Canon Vanstone.[4] I forbear to summarise it because the book as a whole deserves careful and detailed attention. But on the basis of Our Lord's life, Canon Vanstone suggests that it is in seeming defeat, passivity and waiting-for-God that powerful spiritual resources are released. I quote a passage from this book which bears indirectly upon the subject of this chapter:

A bishop of the Church, a man of long and great achievement, became towards the end of his life totally blind and so much afflicted with a number of different illnesses and disabilities that he was confined to bed and almost deprived of the power of movement. He lay supine on the bed, his arms limp, the palms of his hands upwards, so that his very posture suggested his total exposure to whatever might be done to him, his total dependence and helplessness. As one stood beside him on a particular morning some weeks before his death, one had a sudden and overwhelming impression that something of extraordinary significance was going on before one's eyes – something that even surpassed in its significance all that the bishop had done in his years of activity and achievement and service. This impression did not arise from the manner in which the patient reacted to his condition – from any obvious evidences of his cheerfulness or courage; for he spoke hardly at all, and there could be no other expression of his thoughts or feelings. The impression seemed to come, strangely, from the totality of his helplessness and exposure. He was now simply an object exposed to the world around him, receiving whatever the world might do to him; yet in his passion he seemed by no means diminished in human dignity but rather, if that were possible, enlarged.

We began this chapter with a consideration of the difference between St. Matthew's version of the Beatitude and St. Luke's. Luke's version makes no reference to the past and applies the Beatitude exclusively to the present and the future. Whatever may have been the original form, if we may so describe it, Matthew's version of the Beatitude hugely enriches it. In his mind there is a continuum between the Church of his day suffering or threatened with persecution for righteousness' sake, and those who had struggled to come to terms with it in prophecy, in psalmody and in the Wisdom literature. Matthew, like Paul a Hebrew of the Hebrews, finds himself as a disciple of Christ bearing still the burden of the age-old divine vocation. In the sound of the lash and the cry of the bereaved he lives again the sorrows of a Jeremiah, the bitter agony of a Mordecai and the sense of dereliction which accompanied the death of Christ Himself.

I end this chapter with a reference to a classic instance of persecution:

After these events, King Xerxes honoured Haman son of Hammedatha, the Agagite, elevating him and giving him a seat of honour higher than that of all the other nobles. All the royal officials at the king's gate knelt down and paid honour to Haman, for the king had commanded this concerning him. But Mordecai would not kneel down or pay him honour.

Then the royal officials at the king's gate asked Mordecai, 'Why do you disobey the king's command?' Day after day they spoke to him but he refused to comply. Therefore they told Haman about it to see whether Mordecai's behaviour would be tolerated, for he had told them he was a Jew.

When Haman saw that Mordecai would not kneel down or pay him honour, he was enraged. Yet having learned who Mordecai's people were, he scorned the idea of killing only Mordecai. Instead Haman looked for a way to destroy all Mordecai's people, the Jews, throughout the whole kingdom of Xerxes. (Esther 3: 1-6)

In the event this 'pogrom' had a happy ending. Haman himself was hanged on the gallows he had prepared for Mordecai. But for the persecuted there may be no happy ending as the world understands it, only an agonising death and a felon's grave . Nevertheless, they will see the travail of their souls and be satisfied. In this sense, if in this sense alone, those who are persecuted for righteousness' sake are blessed.

*Chapter 13*

# BLESSED ARE YOU WHEN PEOPLE INSULT YOU PERSECUTE YOU AND FALSELY SAY ALL KINDS OF EVIL AGAINST YOU BECAUSE OF ME. REJOICE AND BE GLAD BECAUSE GREAT IS YOUR REWARD IN HEAVEN FOR IN THE SAME WAY THEY PERSECUTED THE PROPHETS WHO WERE BEFORE YOU

This is Matthew's second Beatitude on persecution and it corresponds more nearly than the first to the fourth Beatitude in Luke's version of the Sermon on the Mount. For easy reference I quote again the corresponding passage from Luke:

> Blessed are you when men hate you,
> when they exclude you and insult you
> and reject your name as evil,
> because of the Son of Man.
>
> Rejoice in that day and leap for joy, because great is your reward in heaven. For that is how their fathers treated the prophets. (Luke 6: 22–23)

The similarities are more apparent than real. They have

only two main verbs in common, the words 'blessed' and 'insult'. Once again it is not possible to establish priority of one over the other but I incline to the view myself that the Matthean version is nearer to the original and that the Lukan version has acquired a certain colour and detail from Luke's personal experience of persecution when accompanying Paul on his missionary journeys. For example, the word translated 'exclude' is a quasi-technical word for excommunication, otherwise described in John's Gospel as 'being put out of the synagogue' (John 9: 22; 12: 42; 16: 2). The words translated 'reject your name as evil' were used in the secular world for hissing an actor off the stage. And the 'name' referred to is presumably the name of 'Christian' by which the congregations in Antioch were first known. By the time Luke wrote his Gospel he could well have experienced these particular aspects of persecution which Matthew perhaps had experienced in a different way. Both, however, relate to the life of the early Church in which persecution was conducted not by the State in its official capacity but by the Jewish establishment eager to eradicate heresy from its ranks.

There is another matter which influences the exposition of the passage, and it relates to the literary form in which this Beatitude has been handed down to us.

This particular point is more clearly made in St. Matthew. Whereas the previous eight Beatitudes have been related in the third person – 'blessed are they', etc. – the ninth one is expressed in the second person – 'blessed are you'. Moreover, after a series of short, pithy statements the last Beatitude takes up a disproportionate amount of space in comparison with the others. Some commentators have therefore jumped to the conclusion that the last Beatitude does not properly belong to the series at all, and even if original to Our Lord ought to be treated as a separate utterance. The case against this supposition is well argued by Dr. Daube in his book *The New Testament and Rabbinic Judaism*.[1] For example, this literary form is not an isolated phenomenon and he quotes from a primitive hymn in the Jewish liturgy:

> None is like our God, none is like our Lord, none is like our King, none is like our Saviour.
> Who is like our God, who is like our Lord, who is like our King, who is like our Saviour?
> We thank our God, we thank our Lord, we thank our King, we thank our Saviour.
> Blessed is our God, blessed is our Lord, blessed is our King, blessed is our Saviour.
> Thou art our God, thou art our Lord, thou art our King, thou art our Saviour, thou art he unto whom our fathers burnt the incense of spices.

The last verse of the hymn is longer and also produces direct address. He quotes also from another hymn from Talmudic times:

> Blessed be he who spake and the world existed, blessed be he.
> Blessed be he who was the maker of the world in the beginning.
> Blessed be he who speaketh and doeth.
> Blessed be he who decreeth and performeth.
> Blessed be he who hath mercy upon the earth.
> Blessed be he who hath mercy upon his creatures.
> Blessed be he who payeth a good reward to them that fear him.
> Blessed be he who liveth for ever and endureth to eternity.
> Blessed be he who redeemeth and delivereth, blessed be his name.
> Blessed art thou, O Lord our God, King of the universe, O God and merciful Father, praised by the mouth of the people, lauded and glorified by the tongue of the loving ones and thy servants. We will praise thee, O Lord our God, with the songs of David thy servant. O King, praised and glorified be thy great name for ever and ever. Blessed art thou, O Lord, a king extolled with praises.

There is another more familiar example from Luke's Gospel in which Zechariah's song begins with the traditional 'praise be to the Lord, the God of Israel, because He has come and has redeemed His people' and then changes to the second person halfway through 'and you, my child, will be called a prophet of the Most High; for you will go on before the Lord to prepare the way for him.' Dr. Daube's conclusion, with which I concur, is that:

We may even say that Matthew's transition from the minor key of the third person to the major of the direct address looks more original than Luke's smoother version. In other words, the original series quite possibly consisted of a number of members of equal length and referring to the blessed in the third person – 'Blessed are the poor' – followed by a final member of greater length and addressing the blessed directly – 'Blessed are ye'. On this view, Luke's aim in using the direct address throughout would have been greater evenness of style. We must not forget that passages like the beatitudes were not intended by their authors as dull, academic lists, but as inspiring programmes of a new faith. In those circumstances, to finish an enumeration of 'Blessed are the poor', 'Blessed are the mourners', by a flourish of trumpets, 'Blessed are ye', may well have appeared highly appropriate.

When Dr. Selwyn spoke of 'the philosophy of persecution' he was speaking of it in the abstract as I myself would indeed have to do. I have never been persecuted for the faith or for righteousness' sake. I have enjoyed the privileges that go with an accepted position in society, leadership in the Church and in a community in which Christian values are still on the whole admired, if not assiduously applied. The disciples of Christ had been in much the same position. Galilee was a turbulent place with its own share of riots and rebellions but there is no evidence that they had in their own lifetime suffered for being Jews. Persecution was a thing they read about in their sacred Scriptures but had not experienced themselves.

Dark shadows began to fall across their path when they

became disciples of Christ. Whilst, on the whole, their master was accepted enthusiastically by the people of Galilee, they were aware that the establishment in Jerusalem took a very different view. When they heard one morning that John the Baptist has been executed in prison a shudder may have gone through their minds as they viewed the opposition mounting to their own master. As Our Lord's ministry progressed He began to speak of the sufferings that lay ahead of Him in Jerusalem. When, after some hesitation, Jesus proposed to go to Jerusalem on hearing of the death of Lazarus, it was Thomas, perhaps with a greater sense of realism than the others, who said 'Let us also go that we may die with Him.' (John 11: 16). In St. Mark's Gospel a sense of impending doom begins to dominate the disciples' minds very soon after their ravishing experience of Christ in glory on the Mount of Transfiguration:

> They were on their way up to Jerusalem, with Jesus leading the way, and the disciples were astonished, while those who followed were afraid. Again he took the Twelve aside and told them what was going to happen to him. 'We are going up to Jerusalem,' he said, 'and the Son of Man will be betrayed to the chief priests and teachers of the law. They will condemn him to death and will turn him over to the Gentiles, who will mock him and spit on him, flog him and kill him. Three days later he will rise.' (Mark 10: 32-34)

Jesus did not and could not spare the disciples the prospect not only of His own persecution and death but of the persecutions that would inevitably follow for the disciples if they remained faithful to Him.

> When you are persecuted in one place flee to another. (Matthew 10: 23)
>     I am sending you prophets and wise men and teachers. Some of them you will kill and crucify; others you will flog in your synagogues and pursue from town to town. (Matthew 23: 34)

They will lay hands on you and persecute you, they will deliver you to synagogues and prisons, and you will be brought before kings and governors, and all on account of my name. (Luke 21: 12)

If they persecuted me they will persecute you also. (John 15: 20)

In this world you will have trouble. (John 16: 33)

This was a frightening prospect for men who up to this time had asked for nothing more than to be able to mow their lawns on Saturday, clean the car on Sunday and take the children to school on Monday morning. It is to their eternal credit that when persecution came they withstood it with exemplary courage and faith.

It was right, as St. Paul said, that 'we must go through many hardships to enter the kingdom of God' (Acts 14: 22). This was no 'philosophy of persecution'; it was an utterance wrought out of acute danger and hardship – persecuted from place to place, hounded by the Jewish authorities, imprisoned and beaten, insulted and reviled. Peter and John had already been hauled up before the Sanhedrin (Acts 4), the apostles had been publicly flogged and left the court 'rejoicing because they had been counted worthy of suffering disgrace for the Name' (Acts 5: 41), Stephen, a man full of God's grace and power who did great wonders and miraculous signs among the people, had been stoned to death calling on the name of the Lord (Acts 7: 58), James the brother of John had been put to death with the sword (Acts 12: 2) and Peter had been imprisoned. But the greatest example of persistent heroism and courage still lay in the future. Saul of Tarsus had been himself a persecutor of the Church and had committed many of the believers to prison on a mandate from the High Priest; he had been present when Stephen was stoned to death. But then the persecutor became the persecuted and his epistles abound with reference to the persecution by the very people whose views of the Christian faith he had himself once shared. The Lord's words to Ananias just before Paul's conversion had indeed proved to be true – 'I will sholw him how much he must suffer for my name' (Acts 9: 16).

By the time Matthew was writing some twenty or thirty years later, persecution was endemic in the situation created by the fall of Jerusalem and by the growing animosity between the Rabbinic establishment in Jamnia and the Christian Church. The earlier physical violence to the leaders of the Church in Jerusalem and to Paul in the Diaspora may not have been repeated everywhere where Christians gathered together as a separate congregation, but the possibility was always present. Open contempt, excommunication from the synagogue, slanders, intimidation – all these are reflected in St. Luke's version of the Beatitude. They are suggested, though in less specific terms, in Matthew's version. It was important to be able to say, of some little congregation fearful for their lives or for their property in a little back street in Syria or in a small upper room in Greece, that they were blessed when people insulted them, persecuted them and falsely said all kinds of evil against them because of Christ. They were not only to endure but they were to rejoice and be glad because great was their reward in heaven.

But perhaps the most striking testimony to the sufferings of those early Christians is to be found in a book which is almost exclusively devoted to the 'philosophy of persecution'. The book is the little-understood, much misused book called 'The Revelation'. The book emerges from a background very different from that envisaged either in St. Matthew or St. Luke or even in St. Paul. The earliest persecutors of the new Israel had been the representatives of the old Israel and Paul himself had taken refuge from them by an appeal to the Emperor in Rome. The empire called 'Babylon' in the book stands for the Roman empire of the author's own time which was now persecuting the Christians as Babylon had once persecuted the Jews (see the Book of Daniel). Caligula (A.D. 37-41) had been as mad as a horse but one of his successors, Nero, (A.D. 54-68) was worse, and it was during his reign that large parts of Rome were destroyed by fire in A.D. 64; it was indeed rumoured that Nero had started it himself in order to build something rather more splendid in its place. In order to dispose of the rumour, he found a scapegoat in the Christian minority in Rome and it was in his reign that the first official persecutions began. It is likely that the Book of Revelation was composed or at least completed in the time of Domitian (A.D. 81-96). Whereas Nero had confined his persecution of the Christians to Rome itself, Domitian harassed the Church everywhere in his dominions. It has to be said that the Christians were not the only ones to suffer. It was said of him that you only had to talk to Domitian about the weather to put your life at risk. It was not wholly irrational as in the case of Nero; it became a policy to insist upon the exclusive worship of the Emperor in the interests of imperial unity. Therefore, not to worship the Emperor or to refuse to do so was to open any man to the charge of treason. It was this situation which is reflected in the vivid and sometimes bizarre imagery of the Book of Revelation. The author was a certain John, who was imprisoned on the island of Patmos 'because of the word of God and the testimony of Jesus' (Revelation 1: 9) and the book abounds with specific references to persecution:

Then the angel carried me away in the Spirit into a desert. There I saw a woman sitting on a scarlet beast that was covered with blasphemous names and had seven heads and ten horns. The woman was dressed in purple and scarlet, and was glittering with gold, precious stones and pearls. She held a golden cup in her hand, filled with abominable things and the filth of her adulteries. This title was written on her forehead:

## MYSTERY
## BABYLON THE GREAT
## THE MOTHER OF PROSTITUTES
## AND OF THE ABOMINATIONS OF THE EARTH

I saw that the woman was drunk with the blood of the saints,
the blood of those who bore testimony to Jesus.
When I saw her, I was greatly astonished. (Revelation 17: 3-6)

But the 'blood of the saints' was not to be shed in vain:

After this I heard what sounded like the roar of a great
multitude in heaven shouting:
'Hallelujah!
Salvation and glory and power belong to our God,
for true and just are his judgments.
He has condemned the great prostitute
who corrupted the earth by her adulteries.
He has avenged on her the blood of his
servants.' (Revelation 19: 1-2)

God would be avenged upon the persecutors; 'He will
wipe every tear from their eyes, there will be no more death
or mourning or crying or pain for the old order of things
has passed away.' (Revelation 21: 4). Their redeemer was
coming soon (Revelation 22: 12). 'Blessed are those' he
said, 'who wash their robes, that they may have the right to
the tree of life and may go through the gates into the city'
(Revelation 22: 14). Yes, indeed, the author had seen
everything that Christ had foretold, and more, of the
persecutions that were coming on the earth, and he looked
out from his island prison of Patmos, with the cries of the
persecuted sounding in his ears, with darkness and
hopelessness everywhere around, to the return of the Son
of Man in glory who should put the persecutors to flight
and receive the persecuted into his kingdom. Amen.
Come, Lord Jesus. There are only two words from the
original Aramaic to be found in the New Testament. The

first is *abba* which means 'father'; the second is *maranatha* which means 'Lord come'. Both of them are indications of the frailty and seeming impermanence of the new Israel, persecuted by religious and secular authorities alike. Of them, not just of the old Israel, could be said by the Epistle to the Hebrews:

> Some faced jeers and flogging, while still others were chained and put in prison. They were stoned; they were sawn in two; they were put to death by the sword. They went about in sheepskins and goatskins, destitute, persecuted and ill-treated – the world was not worthy of them. They wandered in deserts and mountains, and in caves and holes in the ground.
>
> These were all commended for their faith, yet none of them received what had been promised. God had planned something better for us so that only together with us would they be made perfect. (Hebrews 11: 36–40)

The Book of Revelation is no 'philosophy of persecution'. It is a heart-cry from a persecuted man on behalf of all the persecuted, of whatever race or creed, invoking the sovereign justice of God against the screaming injustices of men, calling in a new world to redress the balance of the old.[2]

The age of persecution is not over. Indeed it has risen again in unprecedented savagery in our own century – six million Jews at least extinguished in Nazi Germany, and those who survived subjected to nauseating humiliation. What is one to think when Christian pastors in Germany were compelled at gunpoint to walk on all fours and bark like a dog or when Jewish matrons were compelled to climb trees and chirp like birds in the branches. Less obvious, though every bit as well documented, has been the consistent persecution of dissidents behind the Iron Curtain. And even in the West it is by no means unknown for men of a particular colour or race to be discriminated against, or for children to be bullied in school just because they are different, or workers to be victimised at work because they are not prepared to toe the line. Civilisation has not delivered us from the scourge of persecution; it has only served to give it new, more sophisticated and more deadly forms. When every allowance is made for the effect of economic policies or for resurgent nationalisms, there remain huge irrationalities in the 'philosophy of persecution'. No one in his right mind could seriously suppose that the Jews were a deadly threat to the Nazi regime. The Jews of Babylon were no threat to the imperial government, the Christians did not set Rome on fire, the activities of a few heretical sects scarcely endangered the solid structures of the Catholic Church.

It is hard to explain the irrational. There are, however, one or two things that can be said. The first is that the word 'persecution' is nearly always applied, in practice at least, to the activities of a majority against a minority, of a crowd against the individual, of a powerful institution against the occasional dissident.[3] The second is hinted at in the passage previously quoted from the Wisdom of Solomon. I draw your attention now to a short passage from Chapter 2:

> He professeth to have knowledge of God,
> And nameth himself servant of the Lord.
> He became to us a reproof of our thoughts.
> He is grievous unto us even to behold,
> Because his life is unlike other men's, And his paths are of a
> strange fashion. (Wisdom of Solomon 2: 13-15, R.V.)

This is a shrewd observation drawn from the history of Israel. Abel was murdered by Cain because his deeds were righteous, Joseph was intensely disliked by his brothers because of his dreams of glory, Jeremiah was imprisoned and mistreated because he had received a word from God, the unknown subject of Isaiah 53 is victimised by his fellows 'although he had done no violence, neither was any deceit in his mouth'. The unusual girl who is bullied at school, the thoughtful man who is victimised at work, the choirboy in William Golding's novel *Lord of the Flies* are all part of what we might call the 'victim' complex. Over against the victim is what Canetti calls the baiting crowd and I quote from his book (p. 55):

The baiting crowd forms with reference to a quickly attainable goal. The goal is known and clearly marked, and is also near. This crowd is out for killing and it knows whom it wants to kill. It heads for this goal with unique determination and cannot be cheated of it. The proclaiming of the goal, the spreading about of who it is that is to perish, is enough to make the crowd form. This concentration on killing is of a special kind and of an unsurpassed intensity. Everyone wants to participate; everyone strikes a blow and, in order to do this, pushes as near as he can to the victim. If he cannot hit him himself, he wants to see others hit him. Every arm is thrust out as if they all belonged to one and the same creature. But the arms which actually do the hitting count for most. The goal is also the point of greatest density. It is where the actions of all the participants unite. Goal and density coincide.

One important reason for the rapid growth of the baiting crowd is that there is no risk involved. There is no risk because the crowd have immense superiority on their side. The victim can do nothing to them. He is either bound or in flight, and cannot hit back; in his defencelessness he is victim only. Also he has been made over to them for destruction; he is destined for it and thus no one need fear the sanction attached to killing. His permitted murder stands for all the murders people have to deny themselves for fear of the penalties for their perpetration. A murder shared with many others, which is not only safe and permitted, but indeed recommended, is irresistible to the great majority of men. There is, too, another factor which must be remembered. The threat of death hangs over all men and, however disguised it may be, and even if it is sometimes forgotten, it affects them all the time and creates in them a need to deflect death on to others. The formation of baiting crowds answers this need.

The victim is epitomised in the death of Christ. This

famous passion hymn expresses it as well as anything can:

> Sometimes they crowd his way
> and his sweet praises sing,
> resounding all the day
> hosannas to their king:
> then 'crucify' is all their breath,
> and for his death they thirst and cry.
>
> Why, what has my Lord done
> to cause this rage and spite?
> he made the lame to run,
> and gave the blind their sight:
> what injuries! yet these are why
> the Lord most high so cruelly dies.
>
> With angry shouts, they have
> my dear Lord done away;
> a murderer they save,
> the prince of life they slay!
> yet willingly he bears the shame
> that through his name all might be free.

Yes, the writer of the book 'The Wisdom of Solomon' was right – 'he is grievous unto us even to behold, because his life is unlike other men's and his paths are of a strange fashion.'

To explain persecution does not make it agreeable. It was one thing for the disciples to applaud the martyrs of their own race, quite another thing to encounter martyrdom themselves; it is one thing to write a chapter about persecution in the safety of my own study, quite another thing to be compelled to go on all fours and yap like a dog on the concourse of York station. Our Lord does not speak all that much about the rewards in heaven but he does speak about them in the context of persecution. Long before Bonhoeffer stood before a firing squad in the early morning in the prison yard at Flossenburg on 9th April, 1945, he had written these words on the ninth Beatitude:

Having reached the end of the Beatitudes, we naturally ask if there is any place on this earth for the community which they describe. Clearly, there is one place, and only one, and that is where the poorest, meekest, and most sorely tried of all men is to be found – on the cross at Golgotha. The fellowship of the beatitudes is the fellowship of the Crucified. With him it has lost all, and with him it has found all. From the cross there comes the call 'blessed, blessed'. The last beatitude is addressed directly to the disciples, for only they can understand it, 'Blessed are ye when men shall reproach you, and persecute you, and say all manner of evil against you falsely for my sake. Rejoice and be exceeding glad, for great is your reward in heaven: for so persecuted they the prophets which were before you.' 'For my sake' the disciples are reproached, but because it is for his sake, the reproach falls on him. It is he who bears the guilt. The curse, the deadly persecution and evil slander confirm the blessed state of the disciples in their fellowship with Jesus. It could not be otherwise, for these meek strangers are bound to provoke the world to insult, violence and slander. Too menacing, too loud are the voices of these poor meek men, too patient and too silent their suffering. Too powerful are the testimony of their poverty and their endurance of the wrongs of the world. This is fatal, and so, while Jesus calls them blessed, the world cries: 'Away with them, away with them!' Yes, but whither? To the kingdom of heaven. 'Rejoice and be exceeding glad: for great is your reward in heaven.' There shall the poor be seen in the halls of joy. With his own hand God wipes away the tears from the eyes of those who had mourned upon earth. He feeds the hungry at his Banquet. There stand the scarred bodies of the martyrs, now glorified and clothed in the white robes of eternal righteousness instead of the rags of sin and repentance. The echoes of this joy reach the little flock below as it stands beneath the cross, and they hear Jesus saying: 'Blessed are ye!'[4]

But even here and now there are rewards for the persecuted of which we comfortable Christians in the West know nothing, as is evident from the following passage:

Despite the declarations and forecasts of some party members we're living, we grow, we conquer. The trials and persecutions suffered by Catholics in Ukraine have strengthened us even more in the faith and have given us the opportunity to sound the depths of God's providence. I can state without exaggeration that there's nothing greater than to die, a Catholic, in a communist prison. He who loses fear gains truth and hope.[5]

## Chapter 14

# REFLECTIONS

I would like to have been able to dignify this chapter with the title 'Conclusions', but conclusions are hardly to be expected for a subject so enormous in its range and so far-reaching in its implications. So I permit myself only 'reflections' engendered by the preparation for and the writing of this book.

I have been surprised by the extent to which the Beatitudes persistently elude understanding. After many months they remain to me essentially mysterious utterances – at a particular place and time and yet out of the heart of the eternal God. I cannot account for that; I simply record it. Like the Ten Commandments before them they are firmly grounded in history but have a quality of timeless revelation.

I had supposed that I would find ethical and philosophical issues uppermost in my mind in the writing of this book. I have been surprised to discover how seldom they yield positive ethical judgments and how often, on the other hand, they yield spiritual insights into the very nature of reality, human and divine. They are inseparable from the life of a particular man who is known to history as Jesus of Nazareth and whom we honour now as the very presence of God Himself on earth. It has not proved possible to separate the teaching of Christ from the person we believe Him to be.

Timeless though they are, these sayings were earthed in

a political and social environment in which we do not share and of which few of us have any specialist knowledge. But they require for their understanding and exposition some familiarity with that environment – and the imagination to perceive their significance in our own environment, personal and social. If they are to be 'words of life' to our ailing civilisation they have to be seen as relevant to it. They are not and never were intended to be the beautiful utterances of a past age. The word of God is living and active and sharper than any two-edged sword.

I began my detailed preparation of this book just after I retired from York. My defences were down; I was no longer committed to the unceasing activities of the ecclesiastical world. The kind sentiments expressed on my retirement in the diocese and the synod and in many another community in which I had responsibility were now a pleasant memory. I had larger opportunities than for many a year to confront myself as I really was. The Beatitudes spoke to my condition and I did not altogether relish what they said. But as His majesty is, so is God's mercy. His word wounds and heals, disturbs and restores, alarms and consoles. 'No man ever spoke like this man' – this was my reaction to my earliest experience of the living Christ in the R.A.F. during the war. It remains still my reaction after nearly forty years in His service and after a near-lifetime of the study of the Scriptures. I am consumed with awe and wonder at the inscrutable wisdom God has revealed and articulated for us in the life and teaching of Christ.

'Where can we go, you have the words of eternal life.' So said Peter, so have said countless Christians ever since. But these words are not just for Christians and churchmen. They are for the world, and the future of the world depends on the extent to which they are taken seriously and applied imaginatively. Long before a man may feel able to believe in God, to attend divine worship or to embrace the Christian faith for himself, he may begin learning what it means to live by these sayings. To such a person may I say – 'May God deny you peace and give you glory.' It is not part of the 'blessedness' promised to those who follow Christ that they shall be spared mental and spiritual disturbances, but only that a life lived on the basis of these mysterious utterances, however little understood, will give to that life a meaning and a glory nowhere else to be found in this world. I am vividly aware of the imperfections of this book but I shall be more than satisfied if as a result of reading it some seeker after truth may be able to begin his pilgrimage – from the darkened doors of his earthly home to the bright gates of the heavenly city – trusting in these words of life and in Him who uttered them.

# Notes

## Chapter 1

1. Saffrai & Stern, *The Jewish People in the First Century*, Volume II (Van Gorcum, 1976)
2. Mark 3: 21
3. See the book with this title by Sidebotham (Longmans, 1982)
4. John 3: 2
5. Anthony Harvey, *Jesus and the Constraints of History* (Duckworth, 1982)
6. ibid., p. 53
7. See Daube, *The New Testament and Rabbinic Judaism*, Part 2 (Athlone Press, 1956)
8. T. W. Manson, *The Sayings of Jesus* (SCM Press, 1937)
9. Matthew Black, *An Aramaic Approach to the Gospels and Acts* (Clarendon Press, 1971 edition)
10. See Daube, op. cit.
11. Mark 1: 40-46
12. Mark 6: 20, etc.

## Chapter 2

1. For a discussion of this issue, see Allen, *The Gospel According to St. Matthew* (International Critical Commentary, reprinted 1947), LXXIX-LXXXIII.

2. Butler, *The Originality of St. Matthew* (Cambridge, 1951)

3. For the recurrent phrase see Matthew 7: 28; 11: 1; 13: 53; 19: 1; 26: 1

4. M. D. Goulder, *Midrash and Lection in Matthew* (S.P.C.K., 1974)

5. ibid., p. 13

6. Benedict Green, *The Gospel According to St. Matthew* (O.U.P., 1975), pp. 29–31

7. ibid., pp. 27–9

8. G. H. Morrison, *The Wings of the Morning* (Hodder & Stoughton, 1907)

9. Compare Mark 15: 21 – the gratuitous reference to Alexander and Rufus, sons of Simon of Cyrene, who carried the Cross

10. Benedict Green, op. cit., p. 29

11. E. P. Sanders (ed.), *Jewish and Christian Self-definition*, (S.C.M., 1981), Vol. 2, Ch. 10

12. Sandmel, *Judaism and Christian Beginnings* (O.U.P., New York, 1978), p. 359

13. ibid.

*Chapter 3*

1. Jeremias, *Sermon on the Mount* (Athlone Press, 1961), p. 1

2. Galatians 3: 24

3. Harvey MacArthur, *Understanding the Sermon on the Mount* (Epworth Press, 1960), p. 17

4. ibid., p. 60

5. Albert Schweitzer, *The Mystery of the Kingdom of God* (Macmillan, 1954)

6. W. D. Davies, *The Setting of the Sermon on the Mount* (Cambridge University Press, 1964)

7. ibid.

8. Matthew 4: 25

9. Daube, *The New Testament and Rabbinic Judaism* (University of London, Athlone Press 1956), p. 141
10. Martin Buber, *Tales of the Hasidim* (Schocken Books, 1972)
11. T. & T. Clarke, 1904
12. Goulder, *Midrash and Lection in Matthew* (S.P.C.K., 1974)
13. Sandmel, *Judaism and Christian Beginnings* (O.U.P., New York, 1978), p. 359

## Chapter 4

1. N. C. Plummer, *St. Luke* (International Critical Commentary, 1901) and compare Safrai (ed), *The Jewish People in the First Century* (Van Gorcum, 1976), p. 930
2. See S. Blanch, *The Trumpet in the Morning* (Hodder & Stoughton, 1979), Ch. 8 'The Jews Abroad'
3. Safrai (ed), *Jewish People in the First Century*, p. 1058
4. Argyle, *Expository Times*, Vol. 67, p. 92
5. Kittel, *Theological Dictionary of the New Testament* (Eerdmans, 1968), Vol. 4, p. 362
6. *Encylopaedia of Religion and Ethics*, Vol. 2, pp. 675–6
7. Wakefield *A Dictionary of Christian Spirituality* (S.C.M., 1983)
8. Sandmel, *Judaism and Christian Beginnings* (O.U.P., 1978), p. 360

## Chapter 5

1. Hans Kung, *On Being a Christian* (Collins, 1974)
2. Kittel, *Theological Dictionary of the New Testament* (Eerdmans, 1968), Vol. 6, p. 886
3. Hans Kung, op. cit., p. 268
4. Brown, Driver and Briggs, *Hebrew and English*

*Lexicon of the Old Testament* (Oxford, 1939)

5. Kittel, *Theological Dictionary of the New Testament* (Eerdmans, 1968), Vol. 6, p. 892
6. Manson, *The Sayings of Jesus*, (S.C.M., 1949), p. 47
7. D. Bonhoeffer, *The Cost of Discipleship* (S.C.M., 1959), p. 97
8. Sanders, *Jewish and Christian Self-Definition* (S.C.M., 1980)
9. Gaster, *Scriptures of the Dead Sea Sect* (Secker & Warburg, 1957)
10. Vermes, *Jesus and the World of Judaism* (S.C.M., 1983)
11. Manson, *The Sayings of Jesus* (S.C.M., 1949)
12. Goulder, *Midrash and Lection in Matthew* (S.P.C.K., 1974), p. 250
13. ibid., p. 267
14. Emmet Fox, *The Sermon on the Mount* (Harpers, 1934)

*Chapter 6*

1. Farrer, *Matthew and Mark* (Dacre Press, 1954)
2. Hastings, *Dictionary of Christ and the Gospels* (T. & T. Clarke), Vol. 2, p. 208
3. Kittel, *Theological Dictionary of the New Testament* (Eerdmans, 1968), Vol. 6
4. Goulder, *Midrash and Lection in Matthew* (S.P.C.K., 1974), p. 265
5. D. Bonhoeffer, *The Cost of Discipleship* (S.C.M., 1948)

*Chapter 7*

1. Kittel, *Theological Dictionary of the New Testament* (Eerdmans, 1968), Vol. 6, p. 647

2. Gaster, *Scriptures of the Dead Sea Sect* (Secker & Warburg, 1957)
3. See Benedict Green, *The Gospel According to Matthew* (O.U.P., 1975), p. 116
4. Hastings, *Dictionary of Christ and the Gospels* (T. & T. Clarke, 1906)
5. Tugwell, *Reflections on the Beatitudes* (Darton, Alman & Tart, 1980)
6. D. Bonhoeffer, *The Cost of Discipleship* (S.C.M., 1959)
7. Bosanquet, *The Life and Death of Dietrich Bonhoeffer* (Hodder & Stoughton, 1968)

## Chapter 8

1. Isaiah Berlin, *Karl Marx* (O.U.P., 1978)
2. Lionel Blue, *To Heaven with Scribes and Pharisees* (Darton, Longman & Todd, 1975)
3. Kittel, *Theological Dictionary of the New Testament* (Eerdmans, 1964), Vol. 2
4. MacDonald, *Unspoken Sermons*, 3rd Series (Longmans, 1891)
5. Kolakowski, *The Main Currents of Marxism* (Clarendon Press, 1978)
6. MacQuarrie (ed), *A Dictionary of Christian Ethics* (S.C.M., 1967)

## Chapter 9

1. Bible Society, 1984
2. For a fuller discussion of this issue see Blanch, *The Trumpet in the Morning* (Hodder & Stoughton, 1979).
3. Nygren, *Agape and Eros* (S.P.C.K., 1932), Vol. 1, p. 123
4. ibid., p. 124
5. K. E. Kirk, *The Vision of God* (Longmans, 1934), p. 17

6. Nygren, op. cit., Vol. 1, p. 178
7. D. Bonhoeffer, *The Cost of Discipleship* (S.C.M., 1959), p. 101


## Chapter 10


1. K. E. Kirk, *The Vision of God* (Longmans, 1934), p. 25. This is the abridged edition comprising the substance of the Bampton Lectures of 1928.
2. Abelson, *Jewish Mysticism* (Bell & Sons), 1913
3. Harkness, *Mysticism – Its Meaning and Message* (Oliphants, 1973), p. 68
4. See Kittel, *Theological Dictionary of the New Testament* (Eerdmans, 1968), Vol. 3, pp. 430–31
5. ibid., Vol. 3, p. 417
6. K. E. Kirk, op. cit., p. 182
7. Kierkegaard, *Purity of Heart* (Fontana, 1948)


## Chapter 11


1. Published monthly by T. & T. Clarke
2. I. Berlin, *Karl Marx* (O.U.P., 1978)
3. Bauer, *Encylopaedia of Biblical Theology* (Sheed & Ward, 1970)
4. ibid.
5. D. Bonhoeffer, *The Cost of Discipleship* (S.C.M., 1959)
6. P. Petrocokino, *The Heart of it All* (Grosvenor Books, 1983)


## Chapter 12


1. See S. Blanch, *The Trumpet in the Morning* (Hodder & Stoughton, 1979), Ch. 8

2. Selwyn, *The First Epistle of St. Peter* (Macmillan, 1947), Appendix J
3. ibid., p. 301
4. Vanstone, *The Stature of Waiting* (Darton, Longman & Todd, 1982)

## Chapter 13

1. Daube, *The New Testament and Rabbinic Judaism* (Athlone Press, 1956), Ch. 10
2. For a brief but useful introduction to the Book of Revelation see Glasson, *The Revelation of John* (Cambridge University Press, 1965)
3. For an interesting discussion of this particular issue see Canetti, *Crowds and Power* (Penguin, 1973)
4. D. Bonhoeffer, *The Cost of Discipleship* (S.C.M., 1959), p. 103
5. M. Bourdeaux, *The Theology of Persecution* (Speech at Templeton Award Ceremony 1984) Michael Bourdeaux is a Church of England priest and the founder of Keston College, a centre for the study of Religion and Communism.

# THE TEN COMMANDMENTS

## STUART BLANCH

*The value of the Ten Commandments for ordinary people today.*

'I do not regard the Ten Commandments as a burden on our conscience or a restriction of our freedom, but as the God-given way by which, under the guidance of the Spirit, we do God's will, experience His power and see His glory. I look for the dawn which rose that day over Sinai and will rise again over a world healed of its infirmities and radiant with hope.'

*Lord Blanch, former Archbishop of York.*

# THE PRACTICE OF THE PRESENCE OF GOD

## BROTHER LAWRENCE

The conversation, letters, ways and spiritual principles of Brother Lawrence, the seventeenth century French monk who in his monastery kitchen discovered an overwhelming delight in God's presence.

The joy Brother Lawrence found and the deep submission he practised, have made THE PRACTICE OF THE PRESENCE OF GOD one of the enduring spiritual classics. This new translation by Professor Blaiklock includes a substantial introduction setting Brother Lawrence in the context of his time and its thinking, together with an assessment of his teaching.

E. M. Blaiklock, OBE, D Litt, has also translated Thomas à Kempis, THE IMITATION OF CHRIST and is author of many other books.

*A Hodder and Stoughton Christian Classic.*

# THE GREATEST THING IN THE WORLD

## HENRY DRUMMOND

*A devotional classic with a biographical sketch by Denis Duncan.*

The Greatest Thing in the World is the most famous exposition of Paul's Hymn of Love. Love is above faith, says Drummond. It is the foundation of the Christian gospel.

'Some men take an occasional journey into the thirteenth chapter of 1 Corinthians, but Henry Drummond was a man who lived there constantly. As you read what he terms the analysis of love, you found that all its ingredients were interwoven into his daily life'.

*D. L. Moody*

*A Hodder and Stoughton Christian Classic.*

# PRACTICAL PRAYER

## DEREK PRIME

Prayer, asserts Derek Prime, is the most important activity of the Christian life.

In this helpful, clear guidebook, he opens up all the wonder and potential of prayer while looking honestly at the problems. He suggests a structured approach, and reminds Christians that they do not pray in their own strength but with the help of the Holy Spirit. PRACTICAL PRAYER provides clarity and encouragement for all those pursuing the glorious path of prayer.

The Rev Derek Prime is Minister of Charlotte Baptist Chapel, Edinburgh and is author of several books including BIBLE GUIDELINES and CREATED TO PRAISE.